THIRTY YEARS IN THE BATHROOM

Adventures in Urban Education

Pam Carroll

Porcine Publishing

THIRTY YEARS IN THE BATHROOM
Adventures in Urban Education

Copyright 2021

By Pam Carroll

All rights reserved. No part of this book may be used or reproduced in any form or by any electronic or mechanical means including information storage and retrieval system without permission in writing from the publisher, except by a reviewer who may quote brief passages in a review.

Cover Design: Arcane Covers

ISBN: 978-0-578-92846-3 (paperback)

ISBN: 978-0-578-92847-0 (e-book)

Porcine Publishing

Printed in the United States of America

Note: This is a work of creative nonfiction. Events are portrayed to the best of the author's memory. In some cases, characters represent composites of several different people. Names have been changed to protect the privacy of the people involved.

For John

Acknowledgements

Thanks to my girlies: Carol, Diana, Joleigh, and Sheila who showered me with love and support throughout this project.

Thanks to Georgia and the Flowbees, for all their valuable feedback.

Thanks to my students and friends at Baldwin, for inspiring me.

Thanks to John, for being John.

Contents

Thirty Years	1
Before You Mount Up	7
Opening Day	15
Team Teaching	25
Conference Days	37
T.P.	45
A Visit from the Suits	53
Open Mouth, Insert Foot	65
The Substitutes	71
Hell Week	79
Sorry, Wrong Number	89
F Bombs	95
Sexcapades	103
Merde	113
Bobbi's Bodacious Book Pods	123
"I ain't your cuz"	137

Prom Night	145
Deer in the Headlights	157
Field Trip	163
Testing 1, 2, 3	173
Hospital Road Trip	183
True or False	197
Boiled Frog	205
Bits and Pieces	217
Evaluation Day	235
Darryl	247
Cabana Boy	255
Train Story	263
Descent	271
Dog Park	285
Affirmation	293
Home	301

Thirty Years

When my husband John asked me what I was going to call my book, I told him it should be titled *Thirty Years in the Bathroom*. Having lived through those thirty years with me, he understood the title immediately. He thought it was a great idea. "It's an attention grabber," he said. "People will pick it up to see what it's all about."

I'm a retired resource teacher. I spent most of my career at Baldwin High School in an urban school district in Central New York, and yes, I spent the better part of three decades teaching in a converted bathroom. When I moved in, the tile was still on the wall, and the fluorescent lights hung overhead. The four or five toilets and stall doors were removed, and the old plumbing encased in plywood sheets with a little shelf on top. Yes, there were tables and chairs, and even computers, but it was indeed, still a bathroom. Putting lipstick on a pig doesn't turn it into a unicorn.

Why did I work in a bathroom? At that time, Baldwin was home to more than 1600 students, and like schools all over the country, space was at a premium. Very, very few teachers had their own rooms. Most of our teaching staff shared space with a coworker who had an alternating class schedule. Some teachers were in three different rooms, and scurried from place to place pushing a cart full of classroom supplies down the hallway when the bell rang. At least I didn't have to do that. My room was little, but it was all mine.

Next question - what did I do in my little bathroom? I worked with kids who had been identified as having learning disabilities. Many LD kids have typical intelligence, but for some reason, have trouble learning in typical ways, or expressing what they know. They might have trouble with decoding words in a textbook, but they understand the material when it is read to them. Or maybe they can decode the words, but by the time they finish the second paragraph, they can't remember what the first paragraph was about. They may be able to dictate a wonderful essay, but if you ask them to write it down, they expend so much energy in the physical task of writing that they get bogged down and lose the flow of their own ideas. There is a misconnect between what they know, and how well they express it. They need alternate learning strategies to compensate for their disabilities.

Think of it this way. A blind child can't read his history textbook, no matter how much you beg him, or scold him, or - my favorite - tell him he's "not trying hard enough." Teach him to read braille, or give him an audiobook, and he can do it. A deaf child cannot hear the lecture no matter how many times you repeat it. You have to have an interpreter for him. Learning disabilities are like that. These kids are not stupid. People assume they are because many LD kids don't perform well academically, and yet a handicap is not readily visible. Many times a learning disability is not discovered until the child has failed a grade or two. By the time they get to high school, they have faced ridicule, bad grades, and self-doubt. When I was a kid, I used to look forward to going to school. For many of my students, it was daily torture.

My job was to help them cope. Cope with weeding out the bottomless book bag and getting the assignments done. Cope with behavior issues that sometimes arise from a misunderstanding, which, believe it or not, may be rooted in a language disability. Cope with teachers who did not want them in class. Cope with test anxiety. Cope with navigating through a large building with 1600 students on a regular basis.

It occurred to me recently that this whole bathroom thing might be a metaphor for a career in teaching. You have days when you feel like retching. You have days when you feel constipated by paperwork or administrative decisions. You have days when you feel covered in poo, and yes, you have days when you feel refreshed and invigorated.

Thirty years is a long time. Principals and staff come and go. Some of them go very quickly, because the demands of urban education can be grueling. Kids grow up and are replaced by younger faces. They may come back years later with their own children for parent conferences. They remind you that time marches on and that you have touched, and been touched, by hundreds of lives in your teaching career.

The best part of the job was sharing in the kids' successes. I got to watch their smiles form when they finally understood that math formula, or wrote an essay independently, and I got to see them mature from insecure 9th graders to graduating seniors. People would tell me, "Oh, how can you do that? I could never be a teacher." I don't think I could have been anything else.

I loved almost my entire career, but it is certainly not what I envisioned when I played school as a little girl. The daily events of an urban public high school are sometimes so far removed from common perceptions that one might expect to see Rod Serling and a camera crew in a corner of the main office filming an episode of "The Twilight Zone."

I remember telling my friend Stan that someone ought to write these stories down. "No one would believe them." he told me. Hmmm.

Before you mount up

Rita Mae Brown is a prolific author, and she has several different series of books set in rural Virginia. My favorite is her Sister Jane Arnold foxhunting series. Ms. Brown uses a lot of specific vocabulary. To help her readers, she starts each book in this series with a preface of foxhunting terms. In reading her work, I have learned that a *brush* is a fox's tail. A *whipper-in* is an assistant that helps the huntsman by bringing stray hounds back into the pack. A *vixen* is a female fox.

Because the world of education also has a lot of unfamiliar terminology, I realized it might be helpful to start my project with some background information. If it's good enough for Rita Mae, it's good enough for me.

What does a learning disability look like?

There are many different types of learning disabilities, perhaps as many as there are stars in the sky. Dyslexia is the one most people have heard of. Students with dyslexia may have difficulty reading and writing. They may have trouble sounding out words. They may continue to reverse their letters after their classmates have aged out of doing so. Other kids may have dyscalculia, and may have difficulty doing math problems, or memorizing the times tables. Some students may have auditory processing issues which interfere with their ability to interpret what they have heard. These kids almost never get the punchline of a joke. They have great difficulty with multiple step instructions.

All of us have things we do well and things we don't do well. Some of us are visual learners, some are auditory learners, and some are kinesthetic learners. Some people are just better at music than they are at math. A child is identified as learning disabled when IQ testing indicates there is a *significant* discrepancy between his intelligence and his achievement. It is not the same thing as having an intellectual disability, which was formerly referred to as mental retardation.

Think of it this way: if you were hearing impaired and someone read you a story out loud, you would have difficulty answering some comprehension questions. If you could read the story in print, you would likely do much better answering the same questions. It's not about your IQ being impaired. It's about how the information is absorbed and processed.

<u>How is a learning disability diagnosed?</u>

Typically around the time a kid starts learning to read, a teacher or parent will notice a child is having trouble keeping up with his peers. Sometimes disabilities are more subtle, and they don't get picked up until later on. Meetings are held, and testing is done by the school psychologist, who administers an IQ test as well as reading and math achievement levels tests. The psychologist crunches numbers. If a student falls within certain parameters, per the definitions in The Individuals and Disabilities Education Act of 2004, he is eligible for services. Sometimes kids have more than one learning disability, or they have a learning disability and attention deficit disorder. Other times they might be identified as having both a learning disability and an emotional disorder. Or a learning disability and a speech disorder. Lots of times, disabilities piggy-back on other disabilities.

What is special programming?

Special education services cover a wide spectrum. A self-contained class runs like a one-room school house, where the special education teacher is responsible for direct instruction of her students. Class size is reduced and the teacher may or may not have a teacher's aide to assist her. Students in self-contained classes will often be working on material that is several grade levels below that of their typical peers. Some students in self-contained classes have intensive learning disabilities or behavior issues that prevent them from being successful in a typical classroom. Some kids are intellectually disabled or have multiple handicaps. They might have physical disabilities and use wheelchairs. They may or may not be toilet trained. They may or may not use verbal communication. Goals for these kids could include teaching them to become as independent as possible. Some will go on to a type of sheltered employment after leaving high school.

Inclusion kids are *included* in the mainstream. They may spend part of their day getting direct instruction from their special education teacher and then another part of their day in the subject area classes with typical students. Their learning disabilities and/or behavior issues are often less intense than those of self-contained kids. In the last twenty years, there has been a big push to help more inclusion students graduate from high school. At Baldwin, there were some inclusion classes that were co-taught by a special education teacher and a subject area teacher where kids would earn credits toward graduation. Depending on the individual student's ability, inclusion teachers might opt instead to teach a self-contained subject area class that paralleled the subject matter of an inclusion class.

Resource kids have the least intense learning disabilities. Resource students take a course load of typical classes, and then spend one block a day in the resource room. Whereas self-contained and inclusion teachers give direct instruction, resource teachers give supplemental instruction. How one defines supplemental instruction can vary a lot from district to district. In some districts, a student who has a math disability will work only on math assignments with his resource teacher, and a student with a reading disability will only work on improving his reading.

At Baldwin, we were always chasing the almighty graduation credit, so we would help the kids with whatever they needed help with. One day we would work on an

English essay; another day it could be a textbook assignment in Earth Science. We would network with subject area teachers to monitor student progress. At the same time, we would work with students on meeting their IEP goals.

What is an IEP?

IEP stands for Individual Education Program. Students in special education all have IEPS. It is a sort of a yearly lesson plan for students that includes pertinent background information, current academic achievement levels, and goals for the current school year. Special education teachers meet with parents to develop their child's IEP. At Baldwin, we invited the kids to come to their own IEP meetings as well.

What are testing modifications?

Another one of our big jobs was to provide testing modifications for our students. Special ed kids would often have extra time to complete exams. Sometimes they would want directions rephrased so they understood what a test was asking them to do. Sometimes they need a quiet place with few distractions.

How are resource teachers trained?

In addition to required core subjects and state mandated certification classes, I took multiple courses that focused on child development and educational theory. I was very lucky because I spent time in different classrooms from the beginning of my freshman year in college. There are lots of professional conferences available that are helpful as well. Networking with other teachers and getting a mentor when you start teaching is essential. The real learning starts when you go into the classroom.

Ready? It's time to *cast the hounds*. That's foxhunting talk for getting things started.

Opening Day

Opening Day was always exciting. Kids entered the building, dressed in their brand new school clothes, wearing their brand new backpacks, and went to an assigned homeroom for orientation. Each homeroom had two teachers to help students get their ID cards, schedules, and locker combinations. They filled out emergency information cards for the attendance office and the nurse. They went to an assembly and listened to the rules and regulations. After homeroom, they started their classes. It seemed simple enough, but it never worked out that way.

There were kids with no schedules, kids with the wrong schedules, kids with no ID cards, kids with no lockers, and lockers that wouldn't open. Lockers had three different cycles of combinations. The settings were rotated so that one year they were set with the "A" combination, the next year they were set with the "B" combination, and the third year they were set with the "C" combination. One year none of the lockers would open. All the lockers in the building were set to combination "A." All the students were given combination "B." That was a barren source of amusement.

Even though homeroom information had been previously mailed home, there were always changes. Students were instructed to find their name on the list that was posted on the cafeteria window and then go to their assigned homeroom.

Do you remember Woodstock? Have you been on a subway platform in London at rush hour? Or been in line at the Harry Potter ride at Universal Studios? If so, then you can identify with the throngs of students trying to find their names on the displayed lists. It was also a very hot day, expected to go to ninety degrees, with ninety percent humidity, and of course, the air conditioning in our windowless building was not working.

By the time the kids got to homeroom - after they had stopped to chat with friends they hadn't seen all summer - we were, of course, behind schedule. Just as Carla, my homeroom partner, and I got the kids settled, an announcement came over the intercom: "A reminder to teachers, do not send students for schedule changes. Counselors are only seeing students who have *no* schedules this morning. At this time, seniors, please report to the upper football field for your class picture."

Out went a bunch of kids. The senior picture was a tradition none of them wanted to miss, as it was prominently featured in the yearbook, but it interrupted our plans to get paperwork done. Still, we carried on with the rest of the students. There were always a few questions:

"Miss, can I borrow a pen?"

"How do you spell Ticonderoga?"

"I don't know my mother's work phone number."

Monitors were trying to clear the halls. A homeroom next to us went downstairs to the auxiliary gym to have their pictures taken for the yearbook. A few students stopped by to say hello to friends. We shooed them away. Daphne, now a senior, and one of my resource kids, also stopped by. She had a schedule problem. "We'll get it fixed," I told her. "They aren't doing any schedule changes now. Go to your homeroom." She left and disappeared into the crowd in the hallway.

Another group of students went down to have their pictures taken. Then another. Other teachers were sending students without schedules downstairs to get one.

I closed the door and we reviewed the "Baldwin Code of Conduct:"

B   Be respectful

A   Attend all classes

L   Learn something new everyday

D   Do your best

W   Watch your language

I   Invest in Yourself

N   Never Give Up

None of the rules are new, but I thought it was a cute little . . . what is the word for that thing, when the letters represent the words? We moved on to ID cards, and locker combinations. It was getting noisy in the hallway. We checked our itinerary, and realized it was time to go to the auditorium for our assembly, but no one had called us. Still running late, I thought. We punted for a while, and then asked kids about their summer. A young man asked me if he could have his schedule.

I answered, "No, honey, we're going to hand them out after we return from the auditorium. Would you believe some students get their schedule and then leave the building? I'm holding the schedules hostage."

The young man turned to his friend; a bit disgruntled, and said "Oh crap. There goes that idea."

The seniors that left earlier to get their group picture taken returned to our homeroom and we got them caught up. The temperature continued to rise. Carla, hoping to get an idea of how long we would be delayed, went next door to talk with another teacher, who was scheduled for an assembly before we were. Tom's group was supposed to go to the auditorium forty-five minutes earlier, but they hadn't been called yet. The traffic in the halls picked up. It started to look like the midway at The New York State Fair, or maybe the Parade of Nations at the Olympics. I buzzed the office and asked about the assemblies. A secretary answered that we were not moving yet. *Not moving? It seemed to me a lot of movement was going on.* We punted some more. Students began to melt into their chairs. There was a knock at the door. Our principal and police officer entered the room.

"Things are a little busy," said the principal, "so we're doing door to door assemblies."

They chatted for a few minutes about the use of cell phones and the tardy policy. They talked about the Excelsior Scholarship Program that would enable many seniors to go to college with free tuition. They cracked a few jokes with the kids, and then they left. Carla and I passed out schedules, and in a few minutes, it was time to go to the auxiliary gym for pictures. I made a quick stop at the bathroom, and when I got to the gym, I understood why we were so far behind. There were only two photo stations for all those kids. The line extended the length of the Mississippi River.

Finally, homeroom was over and it was time to go to class. Daphne returned to tell me she saw her guidance counselor and her schedule problem was resolved.

"They said they weren't doing schedule changes. How did you get through those lines?" I asked her.

"I don't do lines, Miss," she replied.

I spent class time reviewing individual schedules with my resource kids, checking to be sure they had their required classes. The fire drill alarm sounded. Twice. Twice we exited the building in an attempt to get in some of the required fire drills. More confusion. More noise. My planning time arrived and I headed down to the office, which at this point looked like a triage center. A secretary answered the intercom. "Are they working on the air conditioning?" someone asked her.

Madelyn was one of our guidance counselors, and the head of the department. I wanted to speak with her, but she was standing in the doorway of the office conference room, trying to calm down an irate parent. The mother, the aunt, the family friend, the child, and possibly the attorney were there because of a problem with the child's schedule. Turned out the student with the problem was not even assigned to her, but to Mr. Snake, who was another guidance counselor. Mr. Snake had once again screwed up a kid's schedule, and Madelyn was left to clean up his mess. She summoned him to the office and he arrived just as she was introducing herself to the parent. She explained that she would indeed fix the problem, but the computers had crashed and there was nothing she could do until they came online again. Mr. Snake was defensive and started to talk over the top of Madelyn.

"You," she pointedly said to him, "Sit down and be quiet." She started to close the door to the conference room and caught my eye, realizing I was waiting for her.

"I need to see you about a couple schedule issues, but I'll just put a note in your mailbox."

"Thank you," she answered, rolling her eyes.

Dismissal time arrived. I left my notes for Madelyn, cleared my desk, and grabbed my purse. When I got home and walked in my front door, my husband asked me what I wanted for dinner.

"Valium would be good," I told him. "And chocolate. Lots of chocolate."

Team Teaching

I've always been a straightforward person, so I feel like I should tell you I didn't really spend thirty years in the bathroom. In my day, thirty was the magic number. If you were fifty-five, and you had thirty years in, you could retire with a decent pension. I know the title of the book says thirty years, but technically I taught for more than thirty years, it just wasn't all in the bathroom.

I worked at Lexington Middle School before I moved to Baldwin. They are both in the same district. In the spring of my third year at Lexington I was due for my tenure evaluation. Genie, the special education director from downtown, came to observe me and wrote a very nice report.

She offered a few suggestions and we both signed it. Then she set it aside.

"I want to talk to you about a new opportunity," she told me. "The superintendent has been concerned about the low number of resource students that are graduating from our high schools. A task force of teachers and parents has been meeting with him on a regular basis, and we're going to be piloting a new program at Baldwin next September."

I was intrigued. I listened intently as Genie continued.

"We're adding a resource position. Resource kids and typical kids will be grouped together, half and half, in smaller classes. Classes will be team taught by a subject area teacher and a resource teacher in their core subject areas - English, social studies, math, and science. Ninth and tenth graders will have the support of a resource teacher right in their classroom while instruction is going on. We are hopeful this approach will help more students with the increased work load at the high school level.

"What about the juniors and seniors?" I asked her.

"We lose most of our resource students in their ninth grade year when they turn 16 and are no longer legally required to attend school. Maybe we can expand the program at some point," she replied. "For now, the upperclassmen will get typical resource services as a support period in their schedule."

Looking back, the idea of an integrated "push-in" classroom may not seem so unusual. Lots of resource teachers today pair up with a content teacher to modify the delivery of instruction. But this was the 1980's, and to try it with a whole team of teachers was revolutionary at the time. It had never been done in Baldwin's district before. I didn't know anyplace it *had* been done.

"The subject teacher will be responsible for creating lesson plans and delivering instruction. The resource teacher will be responsible for adapting material to accommodate students' needs. You would be such a perfect fit for the new pilot program," Genie told me. "This will be a new experience for eight people who will have to learn to work together as a unit. Please consider it."

Thus began my adventures at Baldwin High School. Like any new program, we had some growing pains. The first year, I worked with a social studies teacher who got onboard because he wanted smaller classes and a second teacher in the room. He had no interest in modifying his "sage on the stage" teaching style to work with resource kids and there were massive failures. The original science teacher was an egomaniac who knew everything about everything - just ask him. It was indeed helpful for all the students to have two teachers in the classroom so they all got more attention. The downside was that the resource kids on our team suffered because they had no traditional resource period for help with long term projects and completing sticky assignments.

It took us three years to find our groove. The dead weights were replaced by enthusiastic teachers who put the needs of the kids first. Traditional resource time was added to the schedule when the resource teachers volunteered to give up a duty period and teach six classes instead of five. The teachers' union frowned on the idea, as we were working outside of the contract, but it gave much needed support to the resource kids. Roles of who did what in the subject area classroom were negotiated by the pairs of teaching partners. So much of our growth had to do with the generous personalities of the individuals involved. They were a fabulous group of people. We had our issues, but we always worked through them.

We were in a team meeting one afternoon when Maggie, our English teacher, suggested we work together on an "integrated thematic unit." She outlined the process for a group project in which the ninth graders would look for sources and write a research paper. They would work on part of the project in each of the four core subject areas. After some discussion, we agreed that our ninth graders would do a project on endangered animals.

Before the internet came along, students had to use encyclopedias and textbooks and the *Reader's Guide* to find background material. I was in the school library one day, doing some paperwork, when an English teacher brought his class in. He gave some preliminary instructions, and advised his students to select the name of a Greek god from a list he provided. Each student was to write a research paper about a different god. The specific task that day was to find three different sources of information and make photocopies to highlight and paraphrase later. Students who selected Apollo, Atlas, and Aphrodite had no trouble. Students who selected Aether, Amphitrite, and Achelois became increasingly irritable as they wasted valuable time looking for information that did not exist in Baldwin's library. Their teacher told them to pick a different name off the list and they started over. Class ended and they were already behind because they did not have their three sources.

I was determined that would not happen to our team of students. Molly, my science co-teacher, and I would be introducing the project to our team of students. In an effort to find any pitfalls, I spent a week after school with a list of names of endangered animals. After a couple afternoons, Bethany, the librarian approached me.

"What are you working on?" she asked me.

"My team is going to be doing an Endangered Animals project. I'm looking for sources."

"Did you see this new set of books?" Bethany said. "It's a set of encyclopedias, all about endangered animals. Nice short articles, great pictures, good information."

I picked up the C volume and looked for the section on cheetahs. "Oh, this will be a big help," I told her.

"Why are there some names crossed off your list?" she inquired.

"I'm eliminating the animals that don't have three sources readily available," I told her. "I don't want to frustrate the kids."

She stared at me for a moment. "I don't think anyone has ever done that before. Good for you."

My teaching team worked hard to structure the project and build in success. During one English and one science class, the kids went to the library to find and photocopy information including the physical characteristics, habitat, and the reasons their particular animal was endangered. They looked for details about the efforts of different agencies to help preserve their animal. Because I had spent all that time in the library researching the sources, I was able to guide the kids toward materials when they got stuck.

In science class, they created a food web that detailed the predator/prey relationships of their animal. In social studies, they used a world map and shaded in geographic areas where their animal could be found. In math, they made graphs about their animal's declining population. In English, they created an outline, note cards, and a bibliography. A rough draft followed, and then, after corrections, a final paper. The entire process, start to finish, was scheduled to take more than a month, which included time working in class and independently. Teachers around the building were noticing and asking for copies of our lesson plans to use with their own classes. By laying out a step by step process, I thought we had invented a failsafe research assignment. I was perhaps a bit smug about it.

Robert was one of our students, and he picked the African lion as his animal. Like the other kids, he went to the library and found information from an encyclopedia. He *did* have an attendance problem, but he was physically present in multiple classes where vocabulary such as "habitat . . . physical characteristics . . . gestational period . . . predator/prey relationships . . . endangered . . ." was routinely overheard. His classmates were asking questions about animal populations and government attempts at preservation. It was a little disconcerting, therefore, that when Robert began writing his rough draft; it was a wee bit off topic.

"Lion is a city in France. It is located between Paris and Marseille. Lyon is famous for good food. Auguste and Louis Lumière invented the motion picture camera in Lyon. Lion is also famous as the silk capital of the world because it developed an important silk trade with Italy."

How did this happen? How did he get this far into his project without one of us noticing he was so far out in left field? I was flabbergasted. Robert's paper was a topic of discussion when the teachers on our team got together that afternoon for our weekly meeting.

"I do not understand how this happened," I said. I reached across the table and grabbed a chocolate chip cookie off the plate.

"Isn't he the same kid that told us his grandfather had the *Cadillacs* removed from his eyes?" asked Molly.

"No, that was Jack Johnson," replied Peter, another resource teacher. "Don't hog all the cookies. Pass the plate around."

I persisted. "Maggie, the kids do the notecards in your English class. And the outline. I *know* you would have corrected Robert if he had problems then."

"I don't know, Pam," she answered me. "Maybe he wasn't in class then. I could check my attendance book if you want me to. He doesn't have the best attendance."

"That's certainly possible. But still . . . I assume when everyone in your class is talking about lions, and tigers, and bears, you would know you shouldn't be writing a report about a city in France."

Chuck, our social studies teacher, smiled at me. "Never assume." So much for thinking this project was foolproof.

"Maggie is right," said Tim. He was Robert's resource teacher. "His attendance is terrible. And he never brought his paper to my class to get any help. I'll take care of it."

Tim met with him a couple times to help Robert get back on track, and Robert did indeed turn in a fine paper.

The best laid plans of endangered animals and men . . .

Conference Days

The first time I went to a Superintendent's Conference Day I was a very young, very green student teacher. *All* district employees - teachers, administrators, secretaries, nurses, custodians, cafeteria ladies, chief cooks and bottle washers - were sent to a covered football stadium. The superintendent had hired I.M. Brilliant, a nationally-known expert, who was going to tell us all how to save the world of education in a one-day presentation. She stood on an elevated podium on the fifty-yard line in a beautiful brown velvet suit.

"How many of you have read my latest article, *Education is going to a Hell in a handbasket, and only I can tell you how to fix it?*" Disappointed by the small showing of hands raised, she reacted, "You people need to keep up with your professional journals."

As I listened to her, I grew red in the face, until the teacher seated next to me said, "Don't feel bad. The superintendent didn't raise *his* hand, either." Some of the audience zoned out. Some fell asleep sitting straight up. Others read the newspaper. Many did not return after the lunch break. It was a long day.

I guess that early entry into conference days set the tone for me. Let me be clear. I know there are professional organizations that hold forums across town and across the country. I am not talking about *those* conferences. Many people travel to attend them and find them rewarding, myself included.

My favorite conference featured a retired teacher who told her audience that no one had all the answers to the ills of education. She advised us to learn about a variety of approaches, and then pick and choose what was worth trying in our classrooms. I liked her a lot. Another time, I heard the mom of a young man with Tourette's syndrome give a parent's perspective on navigating the landmines of her son's education. I liked her a lot, too.

There were *other* seminars that were built into the school calendar, and were organized and held in-house. In my experience, no one wanted to attend them, no one wanted to be the one to present information at them, and no one started planning for them until the night before they took place. No one found the time away from the students worthwhile.

Spending time at this kind of a conference day is reminiscent of the time John and I went to a local playhouse to see a production of Sam Shepard's *Back Bog Beast Bait*. The show mercifully ended only after the cast turned into beasts and ate each other. There was no intermission and, therefore, no easy chance for escape. John threatened to divorce me when I suggested we start a standing ovation.

Actually, attending this show may have been less painful than attending some of the education programs I have endured. A late August workshop led by Staff Development Coordinator Sally Simpson was particularly painful:

"Hi, everyone, and welcome to today's professional development training. Today we are going to be discussing lesson plans."

Again? I thought to myself. *We're going to reinvent lesson plans again? Didn't we do that on our last conference day?*

"Some of you have heard this before, so I apologize for that. I used to make some adaptations to change it a little, but you probably haven't heard it in six months anyway. I am going to start with designing a unit lesson plan . . . Oh, I guess I need some copies of that paperwork," she said, and left to make copies.

With no one leading the troops, people started leaving the room to grab some coffee or go to the bathroom. The side conversations commenced. Jamila Krisantelli, Vice Principal, popped out of her seat. "Hi everyone, and welcome to today's training workshop. Administrator Kurswell is working on the master schedule of classes. She hopes to have it done a week from Friday. We don't know yet what classes you will be teaching. We don't know when we will know. Hope your lesson planning goes well."

I found her comments rather amusing. *How can we write lesson plans when we don't know what classes we are writing them for?*

Sally Simpson reentered, and passed out copies of the unit plan template. "OK, everyone, we're gonna start by looking at the part that says 'Cognitive Objective.'"

Beverly Richards, English teacher, raised her hand. "Where are you, exactly? I don't see 'Cognitive Objective' anywhere."

"Oh, I didn't like 'Essential Question,' so I changed it to 'Cognitive Objective.' Maybe I didn't fix it on your copies."

Discussion ensued comparing and contrasting the benefits and burdens of Essential Questions and Cognitive Objectives. Sally brought us all back together. "Now we're going to look at another part. Oh wait; I didn't like that part either. I don't like this form."

Beverly continued, "But this is the form we are supposed to use. All of us are supposed to use the same form."

It's the form that the Most Holy carved into the side of Mt. Sinai.

Sally knew she was on the hot seat. "Well, gee, I'm sorry. It's just that I've been on maternity leave and . . ."

I looked around my table. Grace Halloran recognized the form as one she used in Nebraska seven years ago. *Apparently, Mt. Sinai is closer to Nebraska than Central New York.* Tim Carson, another teacher, held his thumb and middle fingers together and began to chant "om." We started discussing where we could go for lunch.

"Now we are going to look at the *daily* lesson plans . . . Oh, I guess I need some copies of that paperwork" Once again, she exited to make copies.

English Teacher Dora Porterhouse wandered around waving a piece of paper. "Did everyone sign in?"

Sign in? How about sign out? How about sign on the dotted line, what's my sign, or the cosine of a right triangle?

First I had better sign up for therapy.

T.P.

My father, a story-telling Irishman with twinkling hazel eyes, lived to the ripe old age of 90. He was a World War II vet - a bombardier in a B-24. I never really understood why that time in his life was so important to him until I went to one of his Army Air Corps reunions in Georgia. I attended a prayer service for those members who had recently died, met some of the men he flew with, and toured the 8th Air Force Museum in Savannah. I listened to some of the stories.

My sister often said that when the last of my father's generation disappeared from the planet, we would hear the vast sucking sound of a great fount of knowledge going with them. These were people who could name all the state capitals, or could tell you if Albania was north or south of

Italy, or convert from quarts to liters without a calculator. They were people you could call in the middle of the night because you needed to go to the emergency room. They were the men and women who came home from the war, got a job, raised a family, and contributed to their community. Tom Brokaw was right when he referred to them as *The Greatest Generation*. That did not, however, prevent them from being creatively snarky when necessary.

If my father was trying to eat a hot fudge sundae, and my brother and I were having an argument, he would tell us that his right to eat his dessert in peace was "one of the things I fought for in the war." If he wanted to take a nap before driving us to the mall, he would say his right to an occasional snooze was "one of the things I fought for in the war." If he insisted on doing the dinner dishes so my mother could take *her* snooze, he would say his right to do the dishes was "one of the things I fought for in the war." It got a little repetitive, but it usually worked for him.

Even years after he died, I heard his mantra in my head when I dealt with the some of the nonsense that went on at Baldwin High School.

One day, at the end of the school year, I went to the ladies' room before classes started. Since it was testing week, I knew I would be very busy, and I'd better go when I could. Unfortunately, there was no toilet paper. Not in the stall, and not in the locker storage area. I made do with some paper towel, and then asked another teacher, our union rep, if she had a key to the custodian's closet. Lo and behold, there was no toilet paper in the closet either. She went hunting, and I went back to class.

Friday afternoon, at the end of that first week of testing, Daphne burst into my room.

"Miss, I have an emergency!"

"What is it honey?"

"There's no toilet paper."

"Oh, that happened to me a couple days ago. Go see one of the custodians."

"No, Miss, I don't need a whole roll. I just need some for myself."

"Oh, that's easy. Just take some of my tissue."

"Thanks Miss. I gotta take a big dump."

I didn't really need to know *all* the details, but to be honest, I do love bawdy humor, and I found Daphne's comments amusing. I spoke with the union rep again, who also had Daphne in her class, and shared the story. She expanded on it. It turns out toilet paper was missing all over the building because "one of the new custodians was stealing it." Preventative measures had been put in place, and it would now be kept in a triple padlocked super-secret hiding place guarded by a raging T-Rex.

It may have been five years later when we once again had another shortage of toilet paper. Due to an ever-shrinking budget, there were no longer going to be boxes of tissue available for classroom use, and we used a lot of it. There was always a kid with an allergy that needed to blow his nose. I just brought in my own supply. It was easy for me because my classes were very small. Some teachers offered kids a free 100 or a one-time homework exemption if they would bring in a box of tissue for their class. Other teachers, including Physics Teacher Tabitha Dawkins, learned to substitute toilet paper for tissue.

I didn't think much about it when I saw her make a run to the women teachers' bathroom and come out with a roll of toilet paper. I went to the same lavatory later that day and noticed the supply was low, but no big deal. Maybe a week later, I saw Tabitha again with another roll. Weird. People started commenting about the low supplies.

Afterschool that day, Vince Sr., one of our custodians popped his head in my room. He was a great guy, and the dad of one of my students. "Do you know anything about the toilet paper disappearing from the women's bathroom?" he asked me. "We had that problem a while ago with one of the new guys, but he isn't here anymore. Somebody complained to the principal. I know I put three rolls in there last night."

The following morning, Tabitha appeared at my door after a pit stop at the ladies' room. Someone had put a long loop of kite string through three rolls of individually wrapped toilet paper, kind of like soap on a rope, and tied them to the post at the top of the stall door. They were accessible, but there were probably a dozen knots at the end of the string. Not much of an anti-theft device, but it made a statement.

There was also a sign posted on the mirror proclaiming that the secret video cameras were on the lookout for a toilet paper thief. Tabitha thought I was responsible for the subterfuge. Hmmm.

"Ok, so what's with the sign in the bathroom?" she asked me.

"Vince got called to the office because there was no toilet paper," I responded.

She was puzzled. "What are you talking about?"

"Vince got called to the office yesterday. Seems a teacher went to use the lav late in the day and there was no toilet paper, so obviously it had to be Vince's fault because he hadn't stocked the lav. Except he *had* stocked the lav, but then *someone* took the toilet paper to their classroom instead of bringing in a box of tissue from home."

My students were arriving and walked around her to take their places in the room. "It's no different than the teachers who take a ream of paper from the supply for the copy machine and use it in their classroom," she countered.

I was getting heated. "Of course it's different. I don't wipe my ass with copy paper. Tabitha, I know you didn't mean to, but you put Vince in the middle of this. That isn't right."

Her demeanor changed. She softened, and recognition dawned in her eyes. "I'll take care of it."

And she did. Tabitha came to see me later to tell me that she had spoken to the principal and then apologized to Vince. I smiled and thanked her. Problem solved.

After she left, I found myself thinking of my father's credo. I wonder if unrestricted access to toilet paper is one of the things he fought for in the war.

A Visit from the Suits

Baldwin had a lot of the same issues that other schools had, but these problems seemed to multiply exponentially in urban areas. Poverty, homelessness, domestic violence, single parent families, crime, drugs . . . they were all roadblocks to education. They were heavy suitcases that our students carried with them when they walked through our doors each morning. They all had an impact on our students' successes. All this negativity caused naysayers to point fingers and assign blame, and committees were formed to address the issues.

Every so often, a group of committee members came by for a visit. They might be administrators from our central office, or an advisory group that sold the district yet another program guaranteed to improve literacy, raise test scores, elevate graduation rates, and grow hair on bald heads.

These "experts" were often people who hadn't set foot inside a public school classroom in umpty-ump years. This did not, however, preclude their ability to divine what was best for our children. Their attention to detail was astounding. They reviewed every atomic sub-particle of extreme minutia. They took furious notes. Then they went back to their offices and wrote reports which proceeded to rip my co-workers and me to shreds.

At a monthly faculty meeting, Principal Len started out by telling us that there would be visitors from the New York State Education Department in the building the following Friday. "Remember folks," he told us, "Last time this group came by for a visit we were written up because some teachers didn't have the daily agenda written on their blackboards. Please be sure to get your agenda up on your board."

A teacher raised his hand. "Len, I don't have a blackboard."

Another teacher called out, "I travel from room to room on a cart. How can I get the agenda up before the kids arrive?"

Len smiled bravely. "I have faith in you."

There was some discussion about using a projector and putting the agenda up on a PowerPoint presentation. *We're spending all this time debating posting a daily agenda?* I buried my nose in my crossword puzzle. Around me there were teachers using their laptops, reading the paper, texting on their cell phones. Anything to escape this drivel. Martin Dawes, philosophy teacher and district attorney wannabe, picked up where he left off at the last faculty meeting:

"In point of fact, Len, research has shown us that posting a daily schedule . . . blah blah blah."

Is it four o'clock yet, I wondered. *Can I leave now?*

In addition to the visitors from the state, the Baldwin

Special Ed Department was due to be audited. The supervisors from downtown's district offices were coming in to be sure that all of our little duckies were happily swimming in a nice neat line. They wanted everything to be perfect before the auditors from the state arrived. Some of the younger teachers were all but panicked.

I was really in no mood for this. John and I had put down our fourteen year old dog a few days prior to the visit and my bullshit tolerance level was set at zero. I knew what worked with my kids. I had decades of experience. I was respected by my administrators, and I was tired of all the histrionics. *Just leave me alone and let me teach.*

Kids in special education classes all have an Individual Education Program (IEP). It is a big packet of information that includes short and long term goals that students have for the current school year. Special ed teachers write new goals every spring and meet with parents to discuss student progress. For one of my resource students, a short term goal might have been to identify the theme of a major work of literature. A long term goal might have been to pass the English Regents.

IEPs came about because in the early days of special programs, there was no accountability. There was little expectation for kids in special programs to graduate from high school. Special classes were held in the basement, next to the boiler room, and it was more or less acceptable for kids to do as little as possible, as long as their teacher kept them quiet.

Fortunately, things changed since the early days and during my time at Baldwin, most of our resource students graduated from high school. Kids attended resource class to get the support they needed in order to be successful in their subject area classes. Sometimes they needed information rephrased so they understood what an assignment was asking them to do. Sometimes they needed drill and practice on the midpoint formula from their algebra class. Sometimes they needed a strategy to help them memorize the elements on the periodic table. The standard approach of the resource teachers at Baldwin was to assist students with *whatever* help they needed.

"Miss, I don't understand this paper."

"What colleges should I look at if I'm interested in Sports Management?

"What's the difference between a simile and a metaphor?"

"How do I sign up to take the SAT test?"

"Do you have a copy of this book on tape?"

If a student came in with a compare/contrast essay assignment, we brainstormed ideas. We made a Venn diagram to show the similarities and differences between the two different concepts. We taught the kids to set up an essay in outline form. We reviewed the use of characterization, theme, and symbolism. We had them check their work for errors and edit for effective vocabulary.

In preparation for the upcoming audit, Baldwin

administrations told us that we needed to start doing "mini-lessons" during resource time. These assignments should be skills based and broad enough so that they would be appropriate for any student. There was nothing wrong with that, but it ate up valuable class time that could be better spent doing classwork that would be graded and turned in for another teacher - work that counted towards their grades and their graduation. This whole mini-lesson idea reminded me of the math lab teacher I knew years ago that would pull kids out of math class to attend math lab so they could work on the math skills that they needed to be successful in math class.

Fortunately, these new assignments would take up only the first 10 or 15 minutes of a 72 minute resource block. Students who were used to having resource time to finish a classroom test or do computer research would still have time to work on these activities.

The other resource teachers and I got together to discuss

the mini-lesson issue. I would write up some brief lessons on proofreading. Theresa would take on graphs and charts. Barbara would do some business math. Steve wanted to address grammar. We came up with a bunch of ideas that we thought were valuable.

The morning of the downtown suits' visit, I wrote the date and the agenda - Today's Lesson: Paraphrasing - on my white board. I had started working with my students when we heard voices outside the door.

"Should I see who it is?" Nell asked me.

"Sure, honey, let them in." I told her. There stood two suits (one male, one female), each holding the requisite clipboard. They were reading some announcements that I had posted on my door. I introduced myself. I introduced the girls. The female suit left. The male suit came in and shook my hand.

"I'm Bart Perkins," he said.

Ooh, the district's director of special education.

I was surprised I didn't recognize him. I had attended a meeting with Mr. Perkins the previous spring. I found him to be ill-mannered and condescending. All too typical of too many suits I had known. He sat down and starting scribbling on his clipboard.

The girls and I took turns reading and paraphrasing items that I had underlined in that day's story. It was a nice little piece I had found online about an unlikely couple named Al and Jeanie Tomaini, who met while they were both working in a circus sideshow. Al was a seven foot giant, and Jeanie, born with no legs, was two feet tall. They had fallen in love and built a life together. Phrases like "embellishment" and "gargantuan" and "acrobatic dexterity" were changed into "stretched the truth" and "gigantic" and "flexibility".

At one point, sophomore Laurie struggled to understand what a "coy" smile was, but she was able to figure it out after I asked her to re-read the previous sentence. The girls had done a good job, and I was proud of them. As the lesson wrapped up, Mr. Perkins asked the girls for their last names. "I want to look at your IEPS later," he told them.

After the mini-lesson was completed, Laurie went on to work on a quiz that her drama teacher had dropped off and Nell pulled out some math homework. I went to my desk and got my lesson plan binder. "I expect you will want to see this," I said to Mr. Perkins.

"Yes, I was just going to ask you for that," he responded. He leafed through it and I asked if he had any questions. "So the first part of the class is a group lesson and then they do their individual assignments?"

"Yes, I answered him. I do a general lesson with them first. Something broad. A skill lesson that they can all find valuable."

"But their goals?" he continued.

"The goal is graduation," I responded.

"Well, yes, but their IEP goals?"

"I address their individual needs through their individual

assignments. I don't pick a day and say today we will work on such and such a goal. I look at the assignments they have to do and address their IEP goals through their assignments. Each kid has a mailbox. Teachers may drop off a project that needs to be completed, or an unfinished test," I explained. "I also create supplemental assignments. Asia, for example, is a senior. She still needs to pass the US History RCT to graduate. We work on parts of that together to help her prepare for the exam. It all shakes out at the end."

He made some notes on his clipboard and left shortly thereafter. Ok, I thought, I'm going to get smacked because apparently I didn't craft their mini-lesson around their IEP goals. Never mind the fact that my administrators had required me to do a *broad-based* lesson. Or that the girls were being successful. Or that the lesson was valuable. Or that they were passing their classes and getting positive reports from their teachers. Or that they were earning credits toward graduation.

While I reviewed my students' IEPS periodically, I didn't have them memorized. Later that day, I had some time to myself, so I looked over the girls' paperwork. I read Laurie's IEP. I read Nell's IEP. Guess what goal was written into both IEPS?

Yep. Summarizing what you have read. Paraphrasing.

Damn, I'm good.

Open Mouth, Insert Foot

My mother was famous for malaprops. She once met one of my father's former teachers. The woman's name was Mrs. Bachelor, but my mother called her Mrs. Husband. The term malaprop, or malapropism is named for a character in a play by Richard Brinsley Sheridan called *The Rivals*. Mrs. Malaprop blunders through the play misspeaking. She uses words that are similar to the word she *intends* to use.

The results of unintentional errors like this can be quite humorous:

"*A witness shall not bear falsies against thy neighbor.*"
Archie Bunker

"I guess I'm gonna fade into Bolivian"

Mike Tyson

"Texas has a lot of electrical votes"

Yogi Berra

"Too many good docs are getting out of the business. Too many OB-GYNs aren't able to practice their love with women all across this country."

George W. Bush

My teaching team and I were also guilty of saying things we didn't really mean on occasion. Molly and I were introducing a ninth grade science lesson about the impact of asteroids on planetary surfaces. The point of the lesson was that if an asteroid was bigger than another one, or if it traveled a greater distance, it would make a bigger crater in the planet's surface. Molly devised a lab where small groups of students used a baking pan filled with flour. The top was sprinkled with paprika. Kids would then drop different objects - a small rock, a big marble, and a tennis ball - from different heights. They would record the diameter of the depressions and graph them. I remember thinking the paprika was a good idea because it made it easier to see the craters against the white flour.

There was always a kid that ended up with flour on his face because he got too close to the pan when the projectile hit, but the kids did a good job and got the idea of the lesson.

On one occasion, the tennis balls were not completely dry before Molly returned them to storage, as the next year when she pulled them out their plastic bags, they were a bit moldy.

"I'm so sorry, class, "Molly said. " I will have to get some new tennis balls. Just look at these moldy balls of mine." I hoped no one would notice her comment, but she went on and on about it. "Maybe I should have rinsed them with Clorox before I put them away. I can't imagine how these balls got so moldy." The girl next to me started to giggle. Then another. Then another. Molly didn't know what she had said until I told her at lunch that day. She was mortified.

Chuck Green had a similar experience in his social studies class. *Toy Story* was very popular in the movies theaters at that time. Burger King was running a promotion and *Toy Story* toys were given out with some of their meals. I was teaching class the day that Roy, one of students, was late to class. Rather than just come in and sit down, he stuck his arm in the door while keeping the rest of his body hidden from view. He was holding Woody, the cowboy.

"Hi, Woody," I said. Woody started dancing in the air. The class laughed. "Come on in. Bring Roy with you," I said.

Roy crossed the threshold, but he was not ready to give up the stage. He continued to wiggle his toy back and forth, thoroughly entertaining the class. Chuck, in an effort to get things back on track, chimed in. "Hi, Roy. Can I hold your

Woody?" Roy's jaw dropped and he gaped at me. I moved close to him, and whispered in his ear.

"Be nice to him, Roy. Mr. Green is an old man. He has no idea what he just said."

The end of the marking period was always a chaotic time. I was very busy one day during a 3rd block class with kids taking tests and finishing projects. Vince, a senior, was working on an essay for his Participation in Government class. One question was about how politicians and the media interact. How do politicians use the media? How are they influenced by the media? How do the media affect the lives of politicians? Vince asked me to explain the question. The Monica Lewinsky scandal had been prominently featured on the news for the last several evenings, so I suggested to Vince that he think about Bill Clinton and Monica Lewinsky, and how the media storm had affected their situation. He thought for a minute and started writing. I turned to another student who was working on a Forensics exam. Jack had a question about carpet fibers. It prompted me to think again about Bill and Monica, and it gave me an idea for another approach.

"Vince, think about the blue dress".

Vince, now fully inspired, began writing so furiously that his pencil lead broke. Tawanda, also present, was working on a math assignment.

"What blue dress? What's with the blue dress?" she questioned.

Vince looked up from his essay. "The President should have been more concerned about being president than about his ejaculatory liquids."

I was astounded by Vince's vocabulary. "Vince," I said. "Wow. I'm impressed. Ejaculatory liquids. That's quite a mouthful." A nanosecond later, my face burned a screaming shade of red, and my students were laughing hysterically.

The Substitutes

Remember your own high school days when students tortured the substitutes? The subs would pass around a piece of paper and ask us to sign in, and we thought we were terribly clever by writing down our pseudonyms: Jacques Strapp, Anne Teak, Jim Shorts, Constance Noring, Jack Cass, and the class couple Lana DeFree and Homer DeBrave.

One day during my senior year of high school Jack Cornwall stood politely behind his desk instead of sitting down. It went on for a few minutes while the sub got organized. Finally looking up, the sub directed Jack to take a seat. Jack politely responded, "I'm sorry. I can't. I have hemorrhoids." We laughed ourselves silly, which of course, disrupted the class. Jack's fellow students were thoroughly entertained. The sub, not so much.

Substitute teachers are in short supply. In urban schools they can be non-existent. There were days at Baldwin when teachers had to give up their planning period to cover for another teacher, and other days when we had to combine classes because there weren't any subs available. The shortage didn't really surprise me. To work in a building where you don't know any of the kids, or the procedures, or the curriculum can be a daunting task. Some of our subs did a fabulous job. They were a godsend and were always busy because they were so highly sought after.

Unfortunately, there were not enough of *those* substitutes. Sometimes we were scraping not the bottom of the barrel, but the dirt u*nderneath* the barrel. *Do you have a pulse? Come be a sub in our district. Don't have a pulse? Come anyway.*

One substitute opened my desk and found two boxes of those really pretty seashell-shaped chocolates that I had received the day before. He ate one chocolate, and then another. He ignored the kids when they told him to stop, and ended up eating both boxes. In for a penny, in for a pound, I guess.

I've known subs who handed out paperwork and sat and read the newspaper instead of working with students. I've met subs who didn't speak enough English to communicate the bare essentials to students, subs who showed up drunk or stoned, and who fell asleep in class. One of the most memorable was the woman who filled in for Keisha Miller, a health teacher.

Tawanda was a junior and one of my resource students. She approached me early one morning. Teachers were getting organized and the bell to first period had not rung yet. "Can I go see Miss Miller before I come to class? I gotta talk to her. I got bounced out of her room yesterday."

"Why did you get bounced out of her room?" I asked her.

"We had a sub. She handed us a packet of work that Miss Miller had left," Tawanda said. "She was telling us what to do, but she talked really fast, and I didn't get it. I think she was from South Africa, or something, because she had a heavy accent. So I told her I was having trouble understanding what she wanted me to do. I asked her, "Can I take this work to my resource teacher's room? I will bring it back later." And she says to me, 'Why are you in RE-source? Are you stupid?' And then I went off on her, and the hall monitor came and walked me to In-School Suspension."

I was beyond enraged. Kids with learning disabilities are accustomed to hearing these comments when they are first diagnosed. I spend a lot of time talking with kids about what a learning disability is, and what it isn't. I work with kids to help them figure out how their brain works best. I try to build self-esteem by teaching them we all have things we do well, and not so well. Mocking a student? In front of a class full of kids? Hurling words like a weapon? It's unconscionable.

I knew Tawanda had a short fuse. "Did you hit her on your way out the door?" I asked.

"I wanted to, but no, Miss. I gotta go explain this to Miss Miller."

"You are not going to see Miss Miller. You are going to see the principal. And I am coming with you."

Tawanda started to fumble. "Miss, it's not my fault. When she said that, I just got so mad I just -"

I cut her off. "You think I am taking you to the principal because I am upset that you had to leave class? You are going to tell your story to him and that despicable b is never going to work in this building again. Not if I can help it."

We went to see the principal and afterwards, Miss Miller. Then we went to see Mr. Warner, who was the vice principal in charge of substitutes. We all knew Tawanda, and knew her to be truthful. She would look you in the eye and tell you to piss off, but she would not lie to you. The personnel office was contacted, and the offender was barred from ever subbing at Baldwin again. I started to calm down.

"Now I gotta go see Mr. Knowles," Tawanda told me, referring to the hall monitor who had escorted her to the in-school suspension room when she had been removed from the class. "I gotta apologize. I used some choice language in front of him."

"Good idea, honey," I responded. "You go ahead. I have to get to class." I was reviewing an essay with another student when she arrived in my room a few minutes later.

"How did it go?" I asked her.

Tawanda smiled broadly. "Mr. Knowles says I used a lot of restraint not to deck her."

"I wouldn't disagree with that," I replied.

Sometimes subs can be overbearing, like the one Tawanda had. Other subs, of course, have different personalities. The whole building was talking about Mr. Jax the day after his visit to Baldwin. Mr. Jax really had no clue how to run a classroom. He had been assigned to a freshman science class. Ninth graders can be very energetic, and their regular classroom teachers sometimes had trouble with them, so it was not really a surprise that Mr. Jax was struggling. He was in over his head. He called the office. An administrator came down, spoke to the class, told them to shape up, and left. Chaos returned. Mr. Jax called again. Another administrator came down, repeated the "shape up" speech, with more rigor and relevance this time, and left. And yes, chaos ensued again. Time passed. Mr. Jax again called the office. This time he was told no one was available. All the administrators were busy dealing with other issues. They would send someone when they could.

Apparently the stress was too much for him. He slumped in his seat. His head hit the desk. The students, apparently concerned, pressed the buzzer and called the office. "You better send the nurse down here. This guy is having a heart attack!"

The school nurse, an experienced career veteran, was calm in an emergency. She arrived in record speed, pushing an empty wheelchair. She approached Mr. Jax, leaned in, and spoke quietly to him. "Can you hear me? How are you feeling? What's going on?"

He popped up. First his head, then his body. He was instantly out of the seat.

"Oh, good, you're here. Now I can leave." And with that, Mr. Jax walked out of the room, down the hall, out of the building, into the parking lot, got in his car, and vroom-vroomed away.

At least he didn't leave the kids unsupervised. Like Tawanda's history sub, he was never seen again.

Hell Week

The second bell rang, signaling the start of class. Tardy students scurried through the hallway to get to their classrooms. I was standing by the door to greet kids as they entered my room. Raul was listening to his Walkman as he turned the corner and hustled down the hall. A moment later, he came through the doorway.

"Mornin' Miss," he said to me. "Sorry I'm a little late. I stopped at the bathroom."

"Mornin' Raul."

He stopped and removed his headphones. "I got some geometry homework I need some help with," he told me. "Graphing circles."

"Oh yes. Using coordinate points and the radius. That can be tricky. I'll see what I can do."

Raul walked past my desk and sat down at a table, joining the other students who had already arrived. Abby, Luther, and Wyatt, all seniors like Raul, were sitting together at a table towards the back of the room. I had known them since they were 9th graders. Jasmine, a petite freshman, sat by herself at a desk.

"It's Hell week, isn't it Miss?" Luther asked me.

"Indeed it is. You should come to the show. Abby is in it."

Abby smiled. "I have three whole lines."

"What's Hell Week?" Jasmine asked.

"Ooooh, time for your initiation!" Wyatt dramatically got out of his chair. "Monday is not so bad, but by Friday, Miss Carroll will be a raving nutcase."

"Oh, Wyatt, stop. I will not." I replied.

"What, this play is gonna be any different from every other play you've done?" he smirked at me.

"It's a musical," chimed Abby. "She'll be worse."

"God help us." Luther shook his head.

Wyatt turned his attention to Jasmine. "I'm just gonna give you a little piece of advice, since you are new here. For the rest of this week, you come to class, you keep your head down, and even if Miss Carroll asks if you need some help, you just say, 'no thanks, I'm good.' If you have a question, ask one of us. Quietly."

"Oh come on, guys, am I really *that* bad?" I looked at Wyatt, and he nodded his head. I looked from Raul to Abby, who smiled broadly, but also nodded. Luther's nose was in his book because he had started his social studies homework, but that didn't keep him from responding to my question with a resolute "Yes, Miss."

Wyatt dramatically fell to his knees. He put his hands together over his eyes and pretended to cry, pitching his voice to an upper register. "Oh, why, did I ever get into this? This is never going to work. I must have been out of my mind. I am never going to do another show again."

I started to belly laugh. His impression of me was a little over the top, but he had the gist of it correct.

My friends Joanne, Deirdre, and I ran the theater program for a while at Baldwin. Typically, Joanne would direct the fall play and I would stage manage for her. We traded these roles for the spring show. Deirdre was our lighting director. Tech Week, or Hell Week, as it is more popularly known, is the final week of rehearsal before a play opens. Trying to explain the stress of Hell Week to someone who has not experienced it is like trying to explain quantum physics to a first grader.

There were so many details that had to come together: costume alterations, scenery touchups, renting the body mics, gathering props, last minute changes in choreography, tech rehearsals with lights and sound effects, musical rehearsals with the orchestra, typing up a program, ticket sales . . . it's no wonder I got a bit testy.

I loved complex scenery and props. During my production of *The Foreigner* I had to have real food onstage for the scenes at the dining room table. While I was frying eggs and making grits for the breakfast scene, Joanne was stopping every night at KFC to pick up fried chicken.

As the finale approached in *Little Shop of Horrors,* a blood-thirsty plant named Audrey II had eaten the entire cast, grown to gargantuan proportions, and moved on to take over the universe. Audrey II was a Venus flytrap about six feet tall. Made of PVC pipes, she was covered in green foam rubber. Every time she ate another cast member - who then crawled through her gullet and out of the hidden exit backstage - the wear and tear on her parts caused her to deteriorate a little more. We were making repairs constantly. Just before the curtain fell, Lighting Director Deirdre climbed onto the catwalk to dangle thirty-foot-long killer plant tentacles over the heads of the audience, threatening to ensnare them. Somehow, the combination of hot glue sticks, prayer, and applause held Audrey II together.

In Joanne's production of *Arsenic and Old Lace,* the Brewster sisters were infamous for poisoning their gentlemen callers with homemade blackberry wine. One night the wine bottle broke backstage, sending Deirdre on a road trip to a nearby restaurant to beg for a replacement. Her car broke down on the way back to school.

"Every year it's the same thing" stated Wyatt. "The actors don't know their lines. The spotlights blow out. The costumes don't fit. Someone has a meltdown. Everyone gets sick."

"How many programs did I fold and stuff for your last show? Five hundred?" Raul asked.

"You said you wanted to help me with that," I replied.

"I lied, Miss."

"I remember that girl that played Emily in *Our Town*" said Abby. "She was such a diva that the rest of the cast threatened to lock her in the dressing room. And the guy that played George? He was always making up or breaking up with his girlfriend. Drama, drama, drama."

"Don't forget about the pig," uttered Luther.

Now Jasmine was intrigued. "The pig?"

"Miss Carroll had a *live pig* onstage. Half the cast wanted to roast him at the cast party, and the other half wanted to rescue him from the pig farmer."

"You really had a live pig?" Jasmine was incredulous.

"When I did *L'il Abner*. He was a very good pig. He was quiet in his crate and he never pooped on the stage. And he was a hit with the audience." I replied.

"Is that why you have all these toy pigs around the classroom?" Jasmine asked.

"Indeed, it is. Most of them were gifts from cast members," I told her.

"What happened to it?" Jasmine asked.

"He went back to the pig farmer." I told her. "And then he went to Oscar Mayer heaven."

"Eeew!" Jasmine scrunched her face.

"Is that the show where your stage manager broke her foot?" Luther questioned.

"She didn't break her foot, she sprained her toes. They got run over by one of the rolling set pieces" I replied.

"Ask her about having the principal onstage," said Abby.

"Oh, come on, now." Jasmine wasn't buying it.

"Same show." I smiled at her. "Mr. Weston played one of the dimwitted Dogpatch husbands. He was barefoot and wore overalls. He was even more popular than the pig."

"How about last year during Hell Week when you called me *an idiot*?" Wyatt inquired.

Jasmine's eyes grew wide. "Miss Carroll called you an idiot?"

"Yes, I did. And I apologized." I responded.

"Nah, Miss, we're good." He turned to Jasmine to explain. "She was having a really bad day and she just lost it. I said something stupid and she told me I was acting like an idiot. I told her there was *only one person* in the room acting like an idiot."

"He was right." I agreed.

"I don't understand," Jasmine said. "If it causes you so much stress, why do you do it?"

"Because it's *fun*," Abby chimed in. "You make new friends. You get really close to the rest of the cast and get up onstage and pretend to be someone else. You work your butt off for two months and you worry that it's not gonna come together but it always does. Opening night arrives and your adrenalin starts pumping and then the audience applauds for you and you are so happy!"

I nodded in agreement. "I always thought doing a show was kind of a metaphor for life." I said. "Doing things you think you can't do. Being scared of failure but moving forward anyway. A group working together for a common goal. It's not just about the show itself. It's about the process."

Fortunately, Raul put all of us back on track. "Miss? Can we get started? You said you would help me with my geometry."

"Sure, Raul."

Wyatt got in a parting shot. "Wait and see, Jasmine. She will be nuts on Friday, and then she will come back here on Monday and say, 'Oh, it was fabulous. Everybody loved it. What show should I do next time?'"

I smiled. Once again, I knew he was right.

Sorry, Wrong Number

Sometimes I think I am the only person on the planet that doesn't like cell phones. I don't want to be constantly available. I don't need to make calls when I am out having dinner with friends, or when I am seated in a public restroom. If you ask me for my cell number, I will lie and tell you I don't have one. The truth is, after a month long *arguescussion* with my husband, I bought a ten dollar TracPhone to make him happy. John believed I should have a phone for emergencies. Every three months I go online and buy another hour to keep it activated. I never use all my minutes.

We have a landline at home which I do not answer if I do not recognize the phone number. God forbid I should agree with the Unabomber, but I think he was right when he said we have become slaves to technology.

In the old days, teachers had limited access to land line phones at Baldwin. There were phones in the main office, of course, but the secretaries were always fielding phone calls from parents, or the district office, or another school, or the superintendent. This made it difficult for teachers to make parent phone calls during the school day. There was a phone in the teachers' lounge that was pretty much in constant use. Sometimes folks went to the library office to use the phone there, but the librarian's phone had a number 3 button that didn't work. You couldn't call anyone who had a number 3 in their phone number. The librarian called the technology department downtown to ask them for a replacement and was told she was number 147 in line for a working phone.

I suspect my disdain of cell phones, or rather, the constant interruption that phones can cause started years ago at Baldwin. In the early days, kids carried pagers. They would keep one in a pocket or backpack, and when the device went off, they would then immediately ask for a pass to the lavatory so they could meander down to the pay phone in the lobby and return the call. *No, honey, you can't go to the lav right now. I'm not deaf.*

Most of the resource rooms at Baldwin were converted bathrooms, and as such, had no intercoms. The main office could not contact the teachers, so landline telephones were installed. I shared a phone line with another resource teacher down the hall. I loved Theresa dearly. She was a fabulous teacher. And several times a week, one or more of her young children, or her husband, would call her, causing the phone to ring in both her room and mine. It drove me nuts. I used to let it just ring, but the noise would reverberate in my tiny bathroom and I couldn't stand it. One of my seniors solved that problem one day when he took the phone apart and put a gigantic glob of masking tape on the ringer so that the phone *couldn't* ring anymore. It purred.

Then cell phones became popular. Kids were told to put them in their lockers during the school day but of course no one did. Every day, teachers fought the battle with students to keep their attention off their phones and on their assignments. Kids texted their friends across the room. They accessed the internet to check their Facebook accounts. My friend Deirdre once had to reluctantly let a student leave her 3rd block Physics class when his mother called to say her check had arrived in the mail. He needed to drive home and take her to the bank.

There was a day that one of my students had a phone ring several times in my room. Bobbi apologized and attempted to silence it, but was having trouble doing so. It rang several more times as she fumbled to turn it off. Finally I picked it up and answered it.

"Hello. This is Bobbi's teacher. She is in class right now and can't talk to you. She will call you back later."

I took a different approach with Brian. He was a very clever young man, with a wicked sense of humor. He had set his phone to vibrate when he came to my room, so it was not going off, but he was clearly distracted by it. When a student has his hands in his lap and seems to be staring at his manhood, you can bet he is texting under his desk.

"Brian," I asked him, "Is your phone being naughty?"

He picked up his head. "What?"

"Your phone. It's being naughty. It appears to be distracting you from your education. "

"I'll put it away, Miss," he replied.

"No, I don't trust it. It needs to go to time out." I extended my hand, palm up, and he reluctantly gave me the phone. I then proceeded to stuff it in my bra. As a zaftig woman, I had plenty of room in there.

Brian stared at me, slack jawed. Normally one with a witty response, he was speechless. His classmates laughed themselves silly. Brian was sufficiently embarrassed. "You can have it back at the end of class. It's gonna stay in the holder for now," I told him.

They all got back to work on their respective assignments. I thought that was the end of it until my boobs started buzzing. My eyes looked down. *What the heck was this?* I wondered. Turns out Brian had borrowed another student's phone when I wasn't looking and texted his own number, causing his phone to vibrate. He started laughing, and so did I. Gotta give him points for creativity.

A few days later, another cell phone went off in another class. "Arthur, is your phone being naughty?" I asked him.

"No, Miss. No," he responded. "I am turning it off right now. I heard about "the holder."

F Bombs

When I was a kid, my mother would unwrap a fresh bar of Lux soap, turn on the water, shove my head in the bathroom sink, and pop the soap in my mouth if she heard me utter the F word. In my parents' generation, speaking this curse probably rated an eight out of ten on the scale of inappropriate behavior for children. But times change. This particular four-letter word has lost a lot of its stigma, and now it is not unusual to hear it in everyday conversation.

Perhaps this is because, grammatically speaking, the F word is very flexible. It can be used to express greetings (*How the fuck are you?*), bewilderment (*What the fuck is going on?*), joy (*That was fucking fabulous!*), and disinterest (*I don't give a fuck.*) It can be a noun (*Why don't you go take a flying fuck?)*, an adverb (*I missed my final exam. I am so fucking screwed)*, and even an interjection (*Fuck! I overslept again.)*

I don't know how many F bombs I heard on a daily basis in the halls of Baldwin High School. It's kind of like asking how many grains of sand are in the Sahara desert or how many snowflakes there are in the Antarctic. I'll put it this way: if we had a cuss jar and charged a quarter for every F bomb that was dropped, we wouldn't need to have bake sales or car washes or bottle drives to raise funds for our extracurricular programs.

It's not that I'm a prude. I've been known to drop an F here or there when I get hot enough. It's just that when you hear it day in and day out, you get tired of the sound of it. If you want to rip into someone, improve your vocabulary, for crying out loud. Get a little more creative:

"I didn't attend the funeral, but I sent a nice letter saying I approved of it"
Mark Twain

"His mother should have thrown him away and kept the stork."
Mae West

"I had a perfectly wonderful evening, but this wasn't it"
Groucho Marx

And my personal favorite:
"I don't wanna talk to you no more, you empty-headed animal food trough wiper! I fart in your general direction! Your mother was a hamster and your father smelt of elderberries!"
John Cleese, as the French Soldier in *Monty Python and the Holy Grail*

Social Studies Teacher Chuck told me a story about the first day of summer school one year. A young man was being disruptive. He didn't want to be spending his summer repeating the class, and apparently he felt compelled to be sure everyone within earshot knew it. After several attempts to verbally redirect the young man to the assignment at hand, Chuck followed up with an unheeded *you-need-to-stop-this-or-you-will-have-to-go* warning. The young man continued his disruptive behavior, at which point ever-steady Chuck approached the student and gently touched his forearm. "It's time for you to leave. Take your things and go to the office. I hope you have a better day tomorrow."

The young man yanked his arm and did indeed proceed towards the exit door, roaring as he left, "Get away from me you fucking faggot! Who the fuck do you think you are? You fucking faggot! Get the fuck offa me! Fucking fucking fucking fucking faggot!"

After the young man left, Chuck turned to the rest of the class and said, "I didn't know it was possible to use the F word so many times in such a brief conversation. Now, back to our lesson . . ."

On another occasion, English Teacher Martha headed to the library during her planning time to make a few copies for an upcoming assignment. She saw a young woman aimlessly wandering the halls. Class had started twenty minutes earlier. The student was moving slowly, texting on a cell phone. She stopped and looked in a classroom window. She waved to a friend. She was apparently in no hurry to get back to class, or perhaps *to* class in the first place. Martha approached the student and asked, "Where are you supposed to be?"

Looking up from her phone, and snapping her gum, the girl responded, "Who the fuck is you?"

When we were told about it later in the teachers' room, another member of her department said, "Martha, you're an English teacher, you should have used the opportunity to discuss subject/verb tenses. The teachable moment and all that. You should have said, 'No, dear. It's who the fuck *are* you? *Who* is the subject. In this case who refers to you. I am, you are, he is . . . so it should be, who the fuck *are* you?' "

Theresa's resource room was down the hall from mine. One day she filled in for Sharon when Sharon (yet another resource teacher) had a parent meeting. Theresa had an interesting interaction with a young lady in the hallway. The very pregnant girl was talking so loudly on her cell phone that the noise disrupted Theresa's class. As the girl was blathering away, Theresa opened the door, approached her and asked, "Where are you supposed to be?"
Unsurprisingly, the girl responded, "Who the fuck is you?"

Being a veteran teacher, Theresa got a little creative and replied, "I'm surprised you haven't heard of me. I am a legend around here."

At this point, overhearing the conversation, one of Baldwin's Vice Principals, Miss Lucy, came out of her office across the hall and ushered the young woman inside, wherein she - the adult in charge - proceeded to screech at the top of her administrative lungs, "Who the fuck are you? Who the fuck are you? You're gonna have a baby and this is the mouth you want your baby to listen to?"

Not having anything pertinent to add to the conversation, Theresa re-entered the classroom and returned to her sub duties.

How utterly fucking unbelievable . . . Oh look! It can also be an adjective.

Sexcapades

I suppose Baldwin was no different from any other subculture when it came to some of the shenanigans that went on. There was the outrageous story of a substitute who turned on the lights at the conclusion of an art class video. He was understandably alarmed to see a young lady on her knees gratifying a young man in the back of the classroom. More than once, different pairs of amorous teenagers were interrupted in a bathroom stall. Certainly we had plenty of students who were sexually active and far too many unplanned pregnancies.

Some of our students viewed having a child while still in high school as a rite of passage. I do remember seeing a couple young girls, both pregnant, fighting with each other in the hall one day when they learned their babies were fathered by the same young man. Seems to me they should have been tag teaming their mutual acquaintance.

Call me naïve, but it *always* surprised me when one of my students came in and started the conversation with "Miss, there is something I need to tell you."

And if the kids surprised me, the adults stupefied me. There was the male occupational therapist who had to hug every woman in the building on a daily basis. There was the archery coach who invited his players to his house to watch porno movies after practice. There was the social studies teacher who flirted openly with the attractive girls. There was the shop teacher who had on-again/off-again relationship with a home economics teacher. When they were off-again, he was involved with a vice principal, but after the *second* child came along, he returned to his first lady friend and married her. The vice principal went on to accumulate multiple notches on her own bedpost from her conquests across the district. One of her liaisons cost her a potential job in another building when the *new* principal turned out to be an *old* paramour.

Then there was Susan - a young, blonde health teacher. I never got to know her very well in the time she was at Baldwin, but my resource students liked her. She was there for a couple years and then got called in to the principal's office just before school started one September. Turned out she was sleeping with the captain of the cricket team. When confronted, she readily admitted to the relationship, but gee, "He is 18, not a minor, and not *my* student, so what is the problem?"

That was the end of Susan's teaching career at Baldwin.

Steven Jacoby was an algebra teacher. I had some resource students that liked him very much and enjoyed his class. He was married with a couple young kids.

Ruth Thompson joined the Baldwin staff one September when an opening came up for a math position at our school.

Steven started out as her mentor, and then at some point, the two of them developed a closer relationship. Personally, I didn't care if Steven wanted to boink a buffalo, provided the buffalo was willing, but he really should have used a little discretion.

Whether we like it or not, teachers are role models for our young adults. There are things we shouldn't do. Don't sit together at every faculty meeting, and don't spend every non-teaching moment in each other's company. Don't wait by the exit in your car while Ruth locks her classroom door so the two of you can leave school in the middle of the day. Don't get caught in a compromising position in her storage closet or in the parking lot by your students. Don't sit on a barstool at the local bar on Friday afternoon with other Baldwin teachers present and have a few drinks while Ruth is standing between your knees. Don't expect your coworkers not to talk.

It was during a 4th block when Serena was working on a project for Steven's class. We had had some issues with multiple fights in the hall, and in an effort to keep the building calm, our principal had made the announcement that there would be no passes issued for the rest of the day. Serena needed something from Steven's room, and she asked me to walk her down there.

"How would Mr. Jacoby feel about your interrupting his class?" I asked her.

"He has a study hall," she told me. "It won't be an interruption."

I knew I wasn't supposed to leave students unsupervised, but my other kids were all seniors and I knew they would be fine. I agreed to Serena's request. We walked downstairs to Mr. Jacoby's room, but he wasn't there. His door was open, students were present - but he was not.

Guess who was covering his study hall?

Ruth explained that Mr. Jacoby had "stepped out" for a few minutes. She was very kind and helped Serena find the construction paper and Xerox copies she was looking for. I walked Serena back to class. She got to work. A few minutes later, a different student asked if I could escort her to the bathroom nearby.

"Don't blow the house up while I'm gone," I told the other students as Lindsey and I headed out. "No wild parties."

Victoria, our hall monitor, was on duty, sitting in a desk at the end of the hall by the girls' bathroom. I liked Victoria a lot. Everyone did. She was an unabashed Christian who exhibited Christian behavior in her daily life. While I was waiting for Lindsey, a call came over her walkie-talkie. Someone was looking for Ruth Thompson. She was needed at a meeting that was in progress. They were desperate to find her. It was Ruth's planning period, so she could be anywhere. They had already checked her classroom. Would Victoria please check in the library?

She started for the library door, but I stopped her. "She's not in the library, Victoria. She's in Steven Jacoby's room. I saw her there a few minutes ago."

Victoria was no fool, and her eyes grew wide. Covering another teacher's class was completely innocent. But Victoria had heard the stories about Steven and Ruth. She could not say anything that would encourage the gossip mongers. "I couldn't tell them *that*," she stammered.

OK, fine, I thought. I took her walkie myself. "Dori, it's Pam Carroll. Victoria is too much of a lady to tell you. So *I'll* tell you. She's in Mr. Jacoby's room."

There was a pause, followed by a sarcastic, "Alrighty, then." I handed the walkie-talkie back to Victoria. Lindsey came out of the bathroom and we went back to class.

The following afternoon, Steven came to see me.

"Your comments yesterday were unfounded and uncalled for"

"What comments were those?"

"Your comments over the walkie-talkie. When you said Victoria was too much of a lady. Your implications."

"Oh. Those comments." I paused a moment to consider my response. *Oh, what the hell.* I took a step toward him and looked him in the eye. "Steven, if you think there is one person in this building that doesn't know what is going on between you and Ruth Thompson, you are mistaken."

"There is nothing going on between me and Ruth Thompson, and your comments are uncalled for." He slithered out of my room. I wasn't really surprised that he had heard about my remarks, but I did wonder how he had heard so quickly.

The mystery was solved when I learned later on that multiple walkie-talkies were all on the same frequency. Any transmission made over a walkie-talkie went to *every* walkie-talkie in the building, and to the district offices downtown as well.

Roger that.

Merde

One of the irrefutable facts of life is that shit is funny. Whether we call it dung or number two or tootsie rolls, we have been laughing about our fecal matter since we wore diapers. One of my students told me about an episode of *South Park* where participants competed to see who could produce the biggest dump on earth. Just the other day our local paper featured a story about two roommates who got in a dispute about poo. Roommate A asked Roommate B to use a fan to dissipate his nasty bathroom odors, as a "common courtesy." Roommate B was offended and proceeded to deposit his kaka on the bathroom floor, in the hallway, and on the leather seats of Roommate A's car.

Fascination with shit extends to the performing arts. Actors are a superstitious lot, and theaters are full of superstitious practices. Don't whistle backstage. Don't speak the name of *the Scottish play* in a theater. Don't put a hat on a dressing room chair. In France, dancers don't say "break a leg." Instead, they will wish each other *"merde"* before going onstage. *"Je vous dis merde"* ("I say to you, shit") or just *"merde"* is a theatrical saying meaning "good luck." One story says that it goes back to the days of the horse and carriage. The more merde in the street outside the theater, the bigger the audience inside the theater. Instead of warning each other to look out for it, performers began to look forward to seeing it as an indication of their show's popularity.

Donny was a freshman when he was working behind the scenes on one of my school shows. Perhaps he was familiar with the theatrical history of merde, because during the final dress rehearsal, he snuck cat turds on the stage. Donny was somewhat disappointed when my stage manager Joanne just cleaned it up with a tissue and rehearsal continued. I think he was hoping for a dramatic reaction, but then, he was an odd kid. It was no big deal. Ralph, on the other hand, was a much more annoying problem.

Ralph was the band director at Baldwin. He was popular with his students and a talented musician. One spring, I was directing a large-scale musical production. On this occasion, Ralph taught the score to the instrumentalists and also played his sax in the pit band. Roxanne, new to our school, was the choral director who taught the songs to the singers. Several weeks into rehearsal, Ralph asked me to stop by the band room during my planning time.

"You need to change the dates of the show," he told me. You need to do it a week earlier or two weeks later." He pointed to the dates on the calendar on his wall.

"Why?"

"You know I have my own band, right? A combo that plays in the community?"

"Yeah." I had no idea where he was going with this.

"We have been asked to play at a local event. It's the same Friday night as the show."

"Ralph, a show has a rhythm to it. You build a show on a seven-week rehearsal schedule and set it up so everything peaks at the right time. If you don't give it enough time, you are under rehearsed. If you give it too much time, it gets stale."

"But I really wanna do this" he whined.

I was getting irritated. "There are probably twenty-five kids in the show. Plus your band kids. Plus the backstage crew, and the lighting director, the choral director . . . You can't ask all those people to change their schedules now. There will be conflicts."

He crossed his arms and looked at the floor. A heavy sigh escaped his lips.

"I'm sorry, Ralph, what you ask is not possible. You signed on to this several months ago. You made a commitment to these kids. You need to honor that."

"Yeah, I guess so," he replied. "I get it."

I thought that was the end of it until our Thursday night performance ended. The show had gone swimmingly. After the hugs and flowers and thundering applause from our audience, I went back stage to lock up the dressing room doors. I was still flying high on adrenaline when Roxanne, the choral teacher approached me.

"I have to talk to you." Obviously distressed about something, she chewed her lower lip.

"Honey, what? You look terrified."

"I really don't want to do this. You're so happy."

"Roxanne, what? What is it?"

"Remember weeks ago, when Ralph suggested that I lead the pit band because he said it would be a good experience for me?"

"Yeah. It was a great idea. You did a great job."

"He set me up. As he was leaving tonight, he told me that he's not coming tomorrow. He has a gig with his band."

I felt blindsided. "What an asshole," I said. "He didn't even have the balls to tell me himself."

Roxanne spoke quickly now. "We'll be OK. He has a sax player coming in to cover for him. I'll make it work."

"Of course you will," I told her. "But the pit band is gonna freak out."

I was, unfortunately, quite correct. On Friday night the band kids, who idolized Ralph, were devastated. It was obvious that he hadn't told them anything. As kids will sometimes do, they vented their anger at the closest person available, who in this case was Roxanne. They snarled at her when she gave entrance cues and reminded them to be silent backstage. The substitute sax player was qualified, but he had never rehearsed with the pit band. Roxanne worked her tail off to hold things together, but when the final curtain fell, she completely dissolved. The stress caught up with her. I found her in her private office. Roxanne had cried so much that her eyes were swelling up.

"Come on, girlfriend" I told her, "we're going out for a beer. Looks like you can use one."

We went to a nearby piano bar and ordered a couple Michelobs. By the time her glass was half-empty, Roxanne was starting to relax. "So," I asked her. "How do you want to handle this?"

"What do you mean?"

"Well, I'm never going to work with him again. I'll hire a professional pit band and pay for it out of my own pocket if I have to. I can't trust him. I'm done," I said.

Roxanne paused to think about my words. She took a long draw on her beer.

"Is there anything you want me to do? Report him to the principal?" I asked.

She put down her drink and stared into space. "I don't know what I want."

The next night, the final night of the show, Roxanne came back and asked me to let it go. She told me that when this was all over, Ralph would still be the band director, and she would still have to work with him. She asked me not to say anything, and I agreed to honor her wishes. Ralph came back to the pit band that night. A role model for passive aggressive behavior, he said nothing to her. Or me. Or the kids. I did my best not to rip out his throat. But I did ponder his crummy behavior. And ponder.

A few days later, I went into my basement and found the Christmas supplies and dug out an old Addis box. Addis was a department store that had the most beautiful gift boxes ever. They were bright gold and shiny, with kind of a basketlike texture, and they made beautiful Christmas packages. I lined the coat-sized box with aluminum foil and plastic wrap, and then I went outside. Wearing a plastic glove, I collected every piece of dog poop I could fit into the box. After I cleared my own lawn, I went to my neighbor's yard. My husband, watching from the front walk, kept yelling "That's enough. That's ENOUGH!" Still, I persisted. When at last I could not squeeze another baby turdlette into my beautiful box, I carefully tucked all the plastic wrap and foil inside. I taped the edges shut.

The following day, I snuck into Ralph's office at school, carefully hauling my very heavy box, and left it on his desk. The gift card read "I wish you merde, you big poopyhead. You deserve it."

I never heard from him about it, but I am sure he knew who had sent it.

Bobbi's Bodacious Book Pods

"Miss, this is impossible. I can't read this whole book. There are too many pages," Bobbi said as she entered my room. She plopped a book on my desk and readjusted her headband, pushing her dark hair out of her face.

Bobbi's English 11 teacher had assigned *Native Son* by Richard Wright. It's a provocative story that generates a lot of discussion, especially in an urban school. Bigger Thomas is a young black man who makes one bad decision after another, but because of the underlying systemic racism, an astute reader will sometimes ponder how much choice he really has.

I knew Bobbi would like the story, but like a lot of kids with reading disabilities, she got bogged down in the mechanics of reading. If she had to read a few paragraphs in a textbook, or a few pages of an assigned reading, she could do it. A full-length book was another story. Bobbi read slowly. She mispronounced words. She had to fight with unfamiliar vocabulary. By the time she finished a paragraph; she had to go back and re-read it. Because she had put so much energy into decoding the words, she had lost the meaning of the text. It was like asking her to walk and chew gum . . . and recite the "Pledge of Allegiance" . . . backwards . . . and in French, at the same time.

"Do you want to try a recorded book?" I asked her. "I can check the public library and see if it's available. It's a well-known book. They probably have it."

"How would that work?" she responded.

"I can order a book on CD. You pop the disc into your CD player and just listen to it. You can even follow along with your own copy of the book."

"I don't know." Bobbi questioned. "It sounds boring."

"I use recorded books all the time when John and I go traveling. A lot of actors read them. Sometimes the authors read their own books. Some of them are really good."

"Yeah, ok, I'll try it," she said.

"If it works for you, we can figure out how to get you a library card of your own and you can order your own books."

I got online later that day and pulled up my local library's web page. They did indeed have *Native Son* available. I placed a hold, and it came in a few days later. Or rather, *they* came in a few days later. All 15 CDs. Bobbi was right, this was a long book. When I saw her in class the next day, she was, understandably, a bit overwhelmed by the volume of the CDs.

"I'll just take two." She told me. "I'll leave the rest with you."

"Good idea," I replied. She carefully wrapped two CDs in tissue and put them in an envelope. Then she was off and running. I stashed the box of remaining CDs in my desk.

Later that day, I went to the office to retrieve my mail. I looked through the papers: a reference to summer school dates, a reminder about an upcoming faculty meeting, a note from another teacher. Piled on the counter were a stack of mini-grant applications. I picked up a copy and glanced at it:

"CALL FOR PROPOSALS: Office of the Superintendent

We welcome you to participate in the annual Creative Instruction Project Mini-Grant Program. This program provides funds to be used for experimental and innovative projects. The focus of the program is to encourage creative instructional practices to improve student achievement. While individual award amounts differ, $30,000 has been allotted to fund creative instructional projects . . ."

I put the application on top of my mail and went to the library to make some copies of progress reports, and I forgot all about it until Bobbi returned to my room two days later for her next class. She bounced through the door with a big smile on her face. Her iPod headphones were in her ears.

"What'cha listening to?" I asked her.

"That book you gave me. You're right. It's a great book!"

"But that's your iPod. The book is on CDs."

"Oh Miss, it was eating batteries like crazy! So I put it on my iPod. It's a lot better. I can listen on my way to school and on my way home. I even listened at lunch today. Other kids just think it's music."

"Ok, speak slowly for the old lady," I said to her. "How did you get it on your iPod?"

"I just downloaded it," she patiently explained. "I downloaded the CD into my computer and then I loaded it to the iPod. Do you have the rest of the CDs? I need to download them, too."

"How many can you download to the iPod?" I asked her.

"All of them. iPods have a ton of space. You could put a bunch of books on here."

The light was beginning to break in my technologically impaired brain. "And you don't need batteries for an iPod, do you?"

"Nope. Just plug it in to the charger at night. Can I use your copy of the book? I left mine home. I want to read along with the iPod in your class today."

My eyes went to the corner of my desk and rested on the mini-grant application. As a light bulb formed over my head, I picked the paper up.

"Bobbi, take a look at this, would you please? The district is offering mini-grants for creative ideas. They are paying up to $1500 bucks for each proposal. What does an iPod cost?"

"It varies. I think mine was about $125."

"How about if you and I write up a proposal for, I don't know, half a dozen iPods, and we load them with a bunch of books . . . all the ones that students need to read . . . *Native Son*, *Of Mice and Men*, *The Pearl* . . ."

"And *Julius Caesar*. Miss, that was the worst."

"And maybe even some books that students want to read on their own . . . *Harry Potter. The Hunger Games. Twilight.*"

"Now you're pushing it," she laughed.

"Will you help me?" I asked her. "I am going to need help with explaining how this process would work."

"Sure, Miss," she replied. "I can do that."

During my planning time later that day, I reviewed the mini-grant paperwork. One of the requirements was a written narrative that addressed a plethora of questions:

"What do you want to do and why? How will this proposal enhance student achievement? If special education students are involved, how will this program meet their IEP goals? What will the students in the program be able to do once they have completed the program? Describe how this project relates to your curriculum. Identify specific NYS Learning Standards and performance indicators that this

project addresses. What are the students going to be doing? Be Specific!! Learning activities must connect directly to the objectives, be enriching and meaningful. How will you determine if the objectives have been accomplished and that student learning has occurred? What plan do you have for sustaining this project beyond this year?"

The questions went on forever. It took some doing, but I got the narrative written in the next few days. Bobbi helped me with the proposed budget page. Then she wrote a letter to the committee describing how she came up with the idea, and why she believed our plan would be beneficial for other students. The cover page required a name for the project. I pondered for a few minutes, and then inspiration struck. I typed *Bobbi's Bodacious Book Pods* in the appropriate space. After making myself a copy of the paperwork, I mailed the packet off to the committee.

The deadline for mini-grant proposals came. And then it went. A couple weeks passed. Bobbi asked me if I had heard anything, which I hadn't, so I crafted a non-threatening email to the head of the committee: *"I know you get lots of proposals and you can't possibly fund them all, but Bobbi was asking so I just wanted to check in . . ."*

It didn't take long to get a response, and when it came, I couldn't call Bobbi fast enough. I tore open my desk drawer; pulled out my address book, and flipped to the V section . . . Velasquez, Roberta . . . She answered the phone on the first ring.

"Bobbi? It's Pam Carroll."

"Hi, Miss. What's up?"

"I heard back from the mini-grant committee about the Book Pods. Do you have a couple minutes? I want to read you their response."

"Yeah, sure. Go ahead," she prompted me.

I took a breath and began to read from the letter I was holding:

Pam,

Oh my goodness . . . I don't know why you didn't get your approval letter (it was mailed to your attention at Baldwin H.S. last week!) The Committee was so excited about your application (and the fact that it was a STUDENT'S idea) that they chose to provide funding for your project for ALL HIGH SCHOOLS. So not only are you getting your grant, but Bobbi's Bodacious Book Pods will be used in all of our district high schools. Maureen Elizabeth Kaufmann, head of the technology department, gave a stirring review of your application . . . I have attached a copy of your approval letter. It was sent through USPS mail (not inter-district) because we've had correspondence go missing through the internal district mail.

But, bottom line . . . CONGRATULATIONS!

We are going to acknowledge your grant application and Roberta Velasquez at this year's Annual Foundation Breakfast, and I will be in touch with more details . . . but make sure you and Roberta have Saturday, April 4th 8:30 a.m.. on your calendars.

Jerry Quint
Foundation Administrator

"So I guess they really liked it?" Bobbi said.

"Liked it?" I replied. "Holy crap on a cracker, Bobbi. They loved it."

She giggled, and I joined her.

"Listen, honey, it sounds like they really want us to go to this awards ceremony they have planned. Can you save that date? It's the first Saturday in April. Probably just a couple hours."

"OK, Miss. If I have to," she replied.

Bobbi and I *did* go to the Foundation Breakfast, along with her mom and grandma. They were smartly dressed for the occasion.

Bobbi wore a running suit over her lacrosse uniform. Her schedule was tight because she had to drive across town for a game after the breakfast.

Bobbi's dad had also planned to go, but got called into work that morning for an emergency. I was sorry he missed it. The event was held in the ballroom of a local convention center. The food was better than average and the tables were set with fine china and linen tablecloths. District bigwigs meandered around schmoozing with each other. I made casual chit chat with Bobbi and her family.

"I'm glad we came," I said to Mrs. Vasquez. "This is quite a party. You must be so proud of Bobbi."

She and Grandma both nodded. "Very proud," she answered.

After the keynote speaker gave her speech, Jerry Quint, the Foundation Administrator, took the stage. He talked about the history of the Education Foundation. He briefly mentioned a couple specific award recipients, and then he turned his attention to Bobbi:

"I've been reading proposals and attending these award ceremonies for years. We've had some really good applications in the past, but this year, we were especially impressed by one of them. It's called *Bobbi's Bodacious Book Pods*. Don't you just love that title? By downloading recorded books onto an iPod, a junior at Baldwin High School came up with a plan to use technology to make books more accessible for students. We liked this idea so much that we are going to be setting up Book Pods in all five of our high schools."

The audience started applauding politely. I smiled at Bobbi. Her mom was near tears.

Mr. Quint scanned the room. "I'd like to ask her to be recognized."

The applause got louder. And louder.

"And I would like to recognize her teacher as well. Roberta, where are you?"

"Bobbi," I leaned in to her. "Stand up."

"What? Miss, no. I can't"

Mrs. Vasquez repeated my request. "Roberta. Stand up. *Stand up.*"

I took her hand. "Do what I do," I told her. I stood, and Bobbi stood up with me. And then I did my best impression of Queen Elizabeth. A gentle smile, a delicate wave of the right hand, from the elbow, not the wrist. Bobbi was beaming. We turned this way. We turned that way. The applause continued for a few moments, and we sat down.

She may have worn a running suit, but it might just as well have been a prom dress and a tiara, because Bobbi was the belle of the ball.

"I ain't your cuz"

Just as things were going swimmingly, a new group of suits from the State Education Department made another visit to continue reviewing the paperwork, procedures, and progress of Baldwin High School. There was a lot of angst in the building whenever they came by, and more than a few humorous anecdotes. Sharon's story was my favorite. She told it to multiple people on multiple occasions, and it got better every time I heard it.

Sharon was a resource teacher on the third floor, and was headed upstairs before the start of classes one morning. Vice Principal Miss Lucy caught up with her in the stairwell.

"They're in your room. Waiting for you."

"Who is?"

"The people from the state. I let them in."

"What? Why would you send them to my room now? Why not send them to a subject area class first, like social studies or English?"

"Because you're the only one who's got her shit together."

Was that a compliment? Sharon opened her door and greeted her guests. About a half-dozen of them. In her tiny little bathroom. They all wore the requisite suits, and carried the requisite clipboards. The men wore ties. The women wore discreet jewelry.

The bell rang. Students started arriving. Big football players. They wore hoodies and had ear buds in their ears. Jamar arrived just before class started and addressed one of the women visitors. "You're in my seat," he told her. She hurriedly scrambled out of the chair, and since there were no other seats left, she stood against the wall. Sharon's mini-lesson of the day was the quadratic formula:

$$x = \frac{-b \pm \sqrt{b^2 - 4ac}}{2a}$$

Here is a quadratic equation for you to try:

$X^2 + 4x - 32 = 0$

First, label the a, b, and c values:

a = 1

It is the number in front of the x squared. Since there is no digit listed, it is has a value of one.

b = 4

It is the second number, the number in front of the x.

c = -32

It is the third number, directly in front of the equals sign.

Then plug the a, b, and c values of the equation into the quadratic formula:

$$x = \frac{-b \pm \sqrt{b^2 - 4ac}}{2a}$$

X= - 4 + the square root of {(4 squared) minus (4 times 1 times -32)} divided by (2 times 1)

X= - 4 – the square root of {(4 squared) minus (4 times 1 times -32)} divided by (2 times 1)

Easy peasy, right?

The quadratic formula is always on the New York State Algebra Regents. Passing that exam is one of the hurdles for graduation. Given their blank faces, Sharon was fairly certain none of the visitors from the state had a clue how to use the quadratic formula. This makes one wonder why it is always on the Algebra Regents, since it is evidently possible to wear a suit and work for the New York State Department of Education and carry a clipboard - without mastering the quadratic formula.

Sharon explained the steps of the formula. She gave concrete directions. *Do the work inside the parentheses first. Do one piece at a time. Watch your positive and negative signs.* The young men worked at white boards posted around the room, first with her assistance, and then independently while she monitored their work and complimented their progress. The suits furiously wrote notes on their clipboards.

After several minutes, there was a loud knock at the door, which then opened. An unknown student appeared in the threshold. He told Sharon he had just had a schedule change, but he was laughing as he said it. It was not unheard of for a Baldwin student to interrupt a class, and then falsely claim he belonged there. Sharon's experienced gut told her that the young man was trying to play her, but Sharon didn't play.

"Yo Miss, I'm in this class now," grinned the visitor. Sharon maintained her composure in front of her guests.

"Young man, sit down at my desk, and I will be with you in a few moments." She returned to her lesson. The stranger was apparently not the patient type, and he persisted, still standing in the doorway.

"Yo, Miss, I ain't got all day."

Sharon turned to face him and repeated herself, more emphatically this time. "I will be with you in a few moments. Take a seat."

The unknown student, still standing, then turned his attention to Jamar. "Yo, cuz, what's up with the bitch?"

Sharon had had enough. "Young man, sit!"

"I ain't no dog" he replied.

Jamar lumbered to his feet. He had had enough, too. "Let me tell you something. I'm a senior, see. I need to pass the Algebra Regents. Miss K. is gonna help me do that. Now, sit the fuck down. Shut the fuck up. Or get the fuck out. And I ain't your cuz."

One can only imagine what the suits were writing on their clipboards at that point. Sharon, inwardly smirking, but understanding that she had to at least *pretend* to address Jamar's threatening tone, put a hand on his shoulder and simply said, "language." He sat back down. The mystery guest chose the last of the three options presented to him and barreled out of the room like a turkey on Thanksgiving morning. Sharon never saw him again, which was just fine with her and with Jamar, who *did indeed* pass the Algebra Regents that year.

(And in case you are wondering, $x = 4$ or $x = -8$)

Prom Night

Baldwin Senior Proms were always a big production. Senior class advisors scouted out local venues looking for a site that was both grand and affordable. The Parent Teacher Organization held multiple meetings to plan the After Prom Party. Girls spent countless hours on websites and at the mall looking for the perfect dress and accessories. Some of the guys would rent a limo and split the cost with a group of friends. Others rented BMWs or Hummers for the night. Once there was even a horse and carriage.

One year, on a beautiful evening early in June, John and I went out to dinner and then headed over to the Metropolitan Hotel for the festivities. Oddly enough, our own prom had been held there many years before. Because we had dressed up for the evening, we got our pictures taken by the prom photographer. We nibbled on some tiny little desserts. At one point, I left John with a couple of my friends while I headed down the hallway to the ladies' room. As I approached the entrance, I saw Grover Weston, my principal, standing there.

"Miss Carroll, I need you to go inside and find out what is happening."

"Is something wrong?" I asked him. Then I heard it. Someone was crying inside. No, not crying. Sobbing hysterically. Now I understood. Grover was concerned because he had heard the sounds of distress.

"Let me know," he said.

I walked into the spacious bathroom and saw Loretta Thompson, Baldwin art teacher, crouching next to an obviously distressed girl who was sitting on the floor in a corner of the room. Her tears streaked through her mascara and eyeliner. She was crunched into a ball with her arms wrapped around her knees and her long dress covering her legs. Loretta spoke quietly to the young woman, her hand placed on the girl's back. I thought I heard the girl say the word "fight" between her sobs. *She got in a fight? At the prom?*

Loretta looked up and we made eye contact. She could see I wanted to talk with her. She patted the girl and then stood up and walked a few steps to stand next to me.

"What's going on?" I said. "Principal Grover is asking."

"This is Corinna. She is a friend of Mariah Dawson."

I was clueless. "Mariah?"

"The girl who had the fire."

My brain clicked into gear. *Fire. Not fight.* A couple weeks before the prom, Mariah Dawson had lost her mother, her sister, and her baby in a house fire. I didn't know her, but I knew her story because the whole school was talking about it.

Loretta continued. "Corinna is feeling guilty. She didn't contact Mariah. She didn't go to any of the services. She couldn't deal with it. Just now she saw Mariah across the room."

"She's here?" I asked. "Mariah came to the prom?"

"I saw her when she arrived," Loretta replied. "She said her mom would have wanted her to come."

Good for her, I thought to myself. "Should we have the girls talk to each other?" I asked Loretta. "Do you think that's a good idea?"

Apparently, someone else had wondered the same thing, because at that moment the door opened again. Loretta and I both looked up.

"Mariah" said Loretta. It wasn't much more than a whisper.

With a laser focus, Mariah scanned the room and saw Corinna on the floor. There was no hesitation, no drama, nothing but pure love emanating from that girl. She approached her friend and sat down on that cold tile floor in her white satin dress and cradled her friend in her arms. "It's

OK," Mariah said. "I know you wanted to come. I love you. It's OK."

I couldn't move. Watching the scene in front of me, I was immobile except for the tears that were spilling down my cheeks. I might still be standing there if we had not been interrupted by the door banging open.

This time it was Jessica, senior girl and daughter of Don Lamberton, a Baldwin English teacher. She was shrieking at the woman who was trailing behind her.

"Why did you come here? You had no right to come here! You are embarrassing me, Mom! You are ruining my prom!"

Her mother? She's talking this way to her mother? I was incredulous.

Jessica went into a stall and slammed the door shut. "Just get out of here! Get out of here!"

If that wasn't bad enough, Jessica's mother started *apologizing* to her ill-behaved child.

"I'm sorry, Jess, it's just that I didn't get home in time to see you in your dress, and I wanted to see how pretty you looked..."

So here I was, standing between the girl who was screaming at her mother, and the girl who had just buried her mother . . . and her sister . . . and her baby. The irony couldn't have been more palpable.

The entry door opened yet again, and another student popped her head inside.

"Miss Carroll? Mr. Weston wants to see you."

I completely forgot Principal Grover was waiting for me. I hurried outside and told him the situation with Corinna had been resolved. Seeing that Jessica's dad worked at Baldwin, I saw no need to mention the mother/daughter drama. The events of that prom would be seared in my memory for a long time.

Fortunately, prom nights with that kind of drama are rare. Most of them go off without a hitch. Sometimes there are humorous happenings that take place.

A few years later, a junior girl named Calamity attended the yearly event as the date of her senior boyfriend. She arrived in a dress made of what appeared to be bridal tulle, with thin strips of gold lame covering the vital areas. It really shouldn't have been tolerated, but it was the first time I knew of that a girl had worn an inappropriate dress to a Baldwin prom. Administrators were caught unprepared, and there were no specific rules against it.

The year after that, we had a new principal. Wanting to avoid any of the dress-code problems he had been told about, Principal Brad preemptively put out a letter to parents explaining that while the school dress code would be relaxed for the prom, anyone showing up in an outfit that was too revealing would not be allowed in the door.

On the Friday night of Principal Brad's first prom, I was upstairs in the ballroom with my friend Deirdre, seated at a round table when Marla, one of our hall monitors made eye contact with me. She approached the table, then leaned in between Deirdre and me and quietly said, "Well, ladies, Calamity has arrived. If you want to get a look at what she is wearing, you best get downstairs now, because there is *no way* that dress is gonna make it into this prom."

Naturally, we thundered down the stairs.

Have you seen pictures of the green dress that J Lo wore? The one that was cut past her navel? It's a circus tent compared to what Calamity was wearing. I had altered a prom dress for one of my students and removed more fabric than Calamity had on. It was long, emerald green, and transparent. There wasn't enough fabric for it to be fitted to her, so it kind of floated over her. The front of the dress had two thin strips of fabric that barely covered her nipples. It was cut so low in front that pubic hair was visible from certain angles. The back was equally low. It wasn't really slit up the side, because there were no sides. The front and back panels were held together with thin tabs of fabric at the bust and hips. That was it.

"Holy shit, would you look at that," I said to Deirdre.

"Ssh" Deirdre replied. "Lower your voice." After gawking for a few moments, we went back to the ballroom.

A few minutes later, Principal Brad came upstairs, perspiring and red faced, and sat down at our table. Grace Goldsmith, one of the senior class advisors came with him. "Oh my God. Her ass was in front of my face!" Brad said.

"What?" I was confused. Brad was breathing heavily. He reached for a glass of water on the table.

Grace filled in the missing pieces. "He offered to let Calamity wear her date's suit coat over her dress. She refused. He offered to let her go home and change. She refused again. Then he told her to leave."

Brad was shaking his head. Grace continued. "Brad walked her to the door, but she stopped short, and then his foot caught her dress . . . and the dress dropped."

"No." My mouth fell open.

"Yes," said Grace. "And she wasn't wearing a bra. Or panties."

The drama continued the next day when Calamity appeared on the local news, wearing her prom dress and bemoaning the fact that she had been unjustly barred from the event. On Sunday afternoon, she was a guest on a local radio talk show and continued her tirade, which did not go well for her. Several folks had seen the newscast featuring the infamous dress the day before and started calling in chastising her.

On Monday morning, the tongues were still wagging at Baldwin. Rumor had it that a mischievous-but-very-talented faculty member gave Principal Brad a Barbie doll wearing a carefully-tailored homemade replica of Calamity's prom dress, which led to nearly everyone in the building bursting into Brad's office demanding to take a look-see. It gave all of us a good laugh.

I wonder who would be clever enough to create a Mini-Calamity doll. Hmmm.

Deer in the Headlights

I was helping Adam with a biology assignment. The shrill pitch of the noise coming from outside my classroom door was ear piercing. Someone was screaming, but it wasn't a human sound. It was more like a wounded animal, perhaps a deer that had been shot and was running for its life, or a raccoon with its foot clamped in a steel trap. I got up out of my chair and opened the door to the hallway. I didn't see anyone, but I heard the footsteps, the uproar getting louder and closer. A female student rounded the corner, plowed into me, and grabbed the collar of my beaded sweater.

"They're trying to kill me," she shrieked in my face. Her eyes were wild, her face contorted. She wasn't really choking me. More like she was hanging onto a life preserver, fearing she was about to go under. Beads from my sweater were spilling on the floor. *Oh good God, what did you take,* I wondered? I went into teacher mode.

"Honey, it's ok. You are going to be ok." She continued to clutch and claw at me. I put my hands on her shoulders. "You're OK, honey. I got you."

The school cop appeared out of nowhere. Probably heard the screaming. Then the student became quiet and her head drooped. I tried to hold her but she was a big girl, and slipped from my hands. She collapsed in a heap on the hallway floor. Lorna, our nurse arrived. Took her pulse. Checked her pupils. *Just breathe,* I told myself. *Lorna's got her now.*

I turned around to return to my room and saw the platter-sized eyes of one of my students. "Are you ok?" Jack, a junior, asked me.

"Not yet. My heart is thumping out of my chest. Give me a minute. I'll be fine." We retreated to the refuge of our classroom and I closed the door. I was anxious to redirect them. "Who needs some help with an assignment?"

Turns out the young lady in question had smoked a joint at lunchtime that was laced with who knows what. She ended up leaving the building that day in an ambulance. She didn't even realize what had happened until the school nurse filled her in when she returned to school a few days later. I was quite touched when she came to my door afterwards to apologize to me. She promised she would "stay the hell away from that stuff" in the future and I gave her a hug. I thought that was the end of that adventure, but I was wrong.

Baldwin had an exchange program with Cadillac High School. Baldwin was urban and impoverished, and Cadillac was suburban and wealthy. Every month pupils from both schools spent a day together, discussing and debating academic and social issues of high school students. Sometimes the Cadillac kids came to Baldwin, and other times the Baldwin kids went to Cadillac. One of my resource kids, Bobbi of the Bodacious Book Pods, was partnered with Kari, a tall blonde senior from Cadillac High. They were both in my class a few days after the aforementioned drama when Principal Brad got on the intercom. He spoke with intensity.

"Attention. May I have your attention, please? I need to discuss an important issue with all of you. We have had a couple of incidents that I need to share with you. A few students have been using some drugs that are very powerful. They cause very bad hallucinations. I don't know what is on the streets this week, but you all need to stay away from it. It will have you thinking that someone is trying to kill you. Seriously, the supply is laced with something nasty and you need to stay away from it. That is all. Thank you."

I'm sure Principal Brad had the best intentions in mind, but the whole thing reminded me of the film footage I had seen in an anniversary special about Woodstock where the concert goers were being told to "stay away from the *brown acid*." It felt surreal.

Cadillac's Kari stared at Bobbi, dumbfounded. I found myself wondering what the conversation would be like at her family dinner table that night.

Bobbi rolled her eyes. "Oh, My God, he did *not* just say that."

I could believe they had drug problems like we did, but I could not believe they had announcements like this at Cadillac High School. I didn't know if I should laugh or cry, so I clamped my jaw shut.

Field Trip

One of my pet projects was educating my students about the nature of their learning disabilities. I've had the same conversation with different kids on numerous occasions. This time it was with Whit, one of my sophomores, and a guard on Baldwin's basketball team:

"I can't do this," Whit said, as he struggled with his geometry assignment. "It's impossible. I'm so stupid."

"You are not stupid. You are learning disabled. We all have things we do well and things we don't do well. If you and I went down to the gym and played a game of one-on-one, who would win?"

Whit smiled. "I would."

I feigned indignation. "You don't think your fat middle-aged teacher can take you?"

Having overheard the conversation, Whit's classmates were laughing out loud.

"I was a good student," I said. "I liked school. But nobody made me take a class in map reading. I would have failed it miserably. Did I ever tell you my staple gun story?"

"I don't think so," Whit replied.

"My husband and I were working at school one Saturday morning with a bunch of theater kids building sets for one of my shows. He sent me to Home Depot to buy a staple gun."

"The one at North and Crestview?" Whit referred to a shop that was probably half a mile from school.

"Yes, that one. Well, I got in my car, I drove down the street, and even though I have been to that Home Depot several times before, I could not find it. I looked for 40 minutes. Finally, I came back to school. I heaved my car keys at my student director. She drove over there and returned with the staple gun in about ten minutes."

LaRhonda chimed in. "Miss, it's like . . . just down the road."

"Yes, it is. I get lost when I am driving all the time. It's infuriating." I continued. "I like teaching, I'm good at it. After you graduate, you can pick a career *you* like, and do what *you* want to do. Right now, you have to jump through a bunch of hoops so you *can* graduate. It's important. It opens so many doors for you."

On other occasions, I taught the kids about functions in the different brain lobes, and Gardner's Theory of Multiple Intelligences. We discussed the differences between auditory, visual, and kinesthetic learners. One spring, when Whit was a senior, a unique opportunity came along. There was a conference at a local country club where Learned Larry was speaking. A nationally recognized professor, author and motivational speaker, he was highly regarded by many people because of his advocacy work for children with learning disabilities.

What made this conference unique is that students were encouraged to come with their teachers. I loved the idea. So did a lot of other people. When I arrived with Whit and a few other seniors who had opted to attend, it was extraordinarily crowded. The organizers opened the conference by saying they had a tremendous response, and they didn't want to exclude anyone.

So here we were, a group of resource teachers and their 400 learning disabled students, some with attention deficit disorders, some with obsessive compulsive disorders, some with emotional issues, and some just plain bored out of their minds as Dr. Larry gave his keynote address and then answered questions . . . for over an hour . . . without a break. He was obviously very knowledgeable, and his speech was affirming for the students, but I believe he was used to giving this seminar to a roomful of educators and hadn't adapted it for his mixed audience.

Dr. Larry finished his presentation, and it was lunchtime. We all moved from the lecture hall to the cafeteria. I snagged a table for my group at the far side of the room. People were lining up for the buffet lunch.

"Aren't you coming, Miss Carroll?" asked Jamie, one of my students.

"You go ahead," I told him. "That line is a million miles long. I'll hold our table and go when you get back."

"OK," Jamie replied. He and Mark, another one of my students, headed for the chow line. I sat and looked over some of the handouts we had received.

My attention was disrupted by the sound of a door banging open and closed. I looked up. I was perhaps fifteen feet away from a fully-extended accordion wall at one end of the cafeteria. The wall subdivided the extra-large dining room into two sections. There were two doors built into the wall, perhaps ten feet apart. Two young boys were chasing each other through the pair of doors in a circular path in front of our table. One of them was wearing a striped shirt, and the other was wearing a plaid shirt. Striped Shirt burst through the first door, slammed it shut, and held it closed by leaning on it. Plaid Shirt then pushed open the door, and chased Striped Shirt as he darted through the other door.

When they came around again, I barked at them.

"Guys!" They stopped and looked at me. "Knock it off. Go get some lunch." They squealed and then darted behind the doors.

"What was that all about?" asked Whit, as he arrived with a towering plate of food. He sat down next to me and dug in.

"They are burning off some pent up energy," I told him. Jamie and Mark reappeared with their own lunches, also piled high and sat down at the table.

"They look so young," Whit said. "Are there middle school kids here?

"I don't know. Maybe."

"You should go get your lunch, Miss," Mark told me.

"Good idea." I replied. I returned a few minutes later with my tray, and then asked, "How did you guys like the speaker?"

"He talked too long, but he had some good - "

Bang! The door slammed again.

I looked up. The two boys were back at it. I got out of my seat this time. I approached them, and raised my voice.

"That's enough. Stop this nonsense. *Now.*" Once again they scattered, this time to the other side of the room, presumably to get some lunch. I returned to my seat and the conversation with my students. *Where is their teacher?* I thought to myself.

Perhaps fifteen minutes later I was drinking a cup of tea while Mark was finishing a piece of cheesecake. It was almost time to head off to the afternoon workshop, which was a panel discussion about how college students with learning disabilities can access academic supports. I was clearing the paper plates off of our table when Striped Shirt and Plaid Shirt reappeared, and the first door slammed once more.

"Oh, for the love of God," I said, to no one in particular.

Whit was on his feet. "Relax, Miss. I got this."

"Yo!" he bellowed, as he strode forward. "I have enough of you and your ignorant bullshit."

The boys scurried behind the second door. Whit positioned himself between the two doors, planted his feet, and crossed his arms. I watched, astonished, as his whole demeanor changed. It was as if he had flipped an internal switch. Somehow he looked bigger. He straightened his back, and he emanated attitude. As expected, the first door opened up again, and in their haste, Striped Shirt and Plaid

Shirt slid directly into Whit. He towered over them, leaning directly into their faces.

"You do not want to piss me off," he quietly said to them.

Well, that was that. This time they flew across the room and out the front door of the cafeteria. Jamie and Mark were guffawing and high fiving Whit as he sat back down. I stared at him, speechless.

He smiled at me. "It's like you always tell us, Miss. We all have things we do well. I can do a real good street thug."

"Remind me not to piss you off," I replied.

Testing 1, 2, 3

Do you remember Pop Rocks? They were a trendy candy in the 1970s. An urban legend warned that you weren't supposed to eat them while drinking Coke, lest you die of a heart attack like Little Mikey of Life Cereal fame. Inside a small black envelope were little red strawberry-flavored clumps that you poured into your mouth where they crackled and sizzled and exploded. That's what final exam time was like at Baldwin. Lots of snapping and hissing that erupted like the chain reaction of a nuclear meltdown. An absolute clusterfuck.

Each of our 1600 students generally had a final exam for each subject. Some courses required two exams: one for the course itself, and one for the New York State graduation requirements. Sometimes instead of a test, there were portfolios assigned, or a lab practicum, or a project, or a class presentation. The rules changed over the years, but often these requirements counted as 25% of a student's final grade. With so much at stake, it was a stressful situation for the kids and teachers alike.

Most of the faculty had five or six proctoring assignments out of 13 testing blocks over a two week final exam period. There wasn't a lot of down time because of all of the marathon grading that had to be done in such a short period. Many of the exams had multiple essays that had to be read and graded by more than one teacher. If there was a discrepancy in an essay score, a third teacher would also have to go over the exam. Then there were final reports to fill out for the district, along with failure notices that were mailed home to parents in time for summer school registration.

Different vice-principals at different times rotated the duty of testing coordinator. It could be nerve wracking. Kids went to the wrong room. Proctors called in sick. Tests were fraught with typos. There weren't enough essay booklets. Or calculators. Or scantron answer sheets. Because of state regulations, Regents exams could not be handed out to proctors until 30 minutes before they were scheduled to begin. It made for a mad rush with many exams to be distributed in a short period of time. It was a lot of pressure, to be sure, which may help explain the behavior of our most infamous and not-so-beloved testing coordinator.

Mr. Harvey was a tall man with piercing eyes and a quite often, a stonewall expression. He took his job as testing coordinator very seriously. A sign on the door to his office said *"Testing Center. Do not enter."* He had neat little piles of tests on his desk. At precisely T- minus 30 minutes to test time, his door opened, and he barked at the first person in line. A test proctor would step into the room and carefully follow the established procedure. State the name of the test, the teacher of record, and the class period you are proctoring for. Extend your arms for your pile of tests, and then wait . . . silently. No questions allowed. Do not make eye contact. Do not attempt to help the testing coordinator look for your tests. And for God's sake, do not distract him with questions about extra scrap paper, tomorrow's test, or changing a proctoring assignment. Worse than that, if you are next in line, *do not under any circumstances cross the threshold into the testing office*. You will not get your tests, you will be sent to the end of the line, and you may lose a reproductive organ.

Seinfeld was a popular sitcom on TV in those days. Because Mr. Harvey's rigid protocol was similar to the infamous Soup Nazi character on that program, he became known among the Baldwin staff as the Test Nazi. Honestly though, I think he was proud of that reputation. On one occasion, after he and I had our own little . . . skirmish, I bought him a small gift. I didn't feel right ordering him any

Nazi paraphernalia, so I got him a necktie. It was black with little green Dr. Seuss' Grinches scattered all over it. He wore it proudly that day, and for every subsequent testing day after that.

At one point, Mr. Harvey was also the special education administrator at Baldwin, and another one of his jobs was to secure additional proctors for the resource kids at Baldwin. Our resource students had testing modifications, including extra time and/or a separate location. They could take their exams with their own resource teacher, or another resource teacher, or a proctor in a small, quiet place instead of the larger classroom setting where they might have been easily distracted. Some resource students could use a calculator. Some had a scribe to record their answers for them. Some could have the test read aloud to them. It all depended on the individual student and the specific disability.

Exam blocks started at either 8:30 in the morning or 12:30 in the afternoon. They were three hours long, but because some resource students had double time for a test, there were occasions when new students arrived for afternoon exams and students from morning exams would still be there.

Sometimes during testing week, one or more resource teachers would be working until 6:30 pm. Because our students took a wide variety of classes, we were proctoring almost every testing session. There were days I didn't take a break, so John always packed me an extra nice lunch. I made it a point not to drink too much coffee in the morning to cut down on trips to the ladies' room.

Some of our extra readers were terrific at working individually with kids. Specific students would request specific readers from time to time. Other readers were not as good. Once during an arduous English Regents, I requested a floater to be assigned to the six resource teachers. My thought was that the floater could travel between the different groups to check in and see if anyone needed a bathroom break, or a short walk to clear his head.

Even though one of our guidance counselors, Mr. Snake, was previously given a copy of the proctoring schedule, he never showed up to my room. I called the main office after two and a half hours to have him hunted down, and he arrived at my door soon afterwards, saying, "Oh, sorry...." At the end of the day, a secretary told me she had found him taking a nap in his office.

Mr. Snake took a couple of my young ladies for a walk to the potty, and then I asked him to supervise the kids while I did likewise. When I returned, I found him loudly talking on his cell phone in the hallway outside my door. When I shared this little tidbit with another resource teacher, she told me that he once had been assigned as reader for one of her students. Despite her specific instructions, Mr. Snake spent his time as a reader reading the newspaper while the kid took the test.

Irresponsible proctors like him drove me batty. So did the constant interruptions. I hung a sign on my door that politely requested we not be disturbed because we were testing. Unfortunately, this did not prevent multiple *allegedly* professional adults from entering my room during testing for the most inane reasons: *Do you want to go to lunch today? Do you have any copies of those end-of-the-year forms? Do you have any extra pens? Can I use your phone? Do you know where Mrs. So and So went?*

Remembering the days when our cat Mr. Bibbles would get on the kitchen counters, I pondered the possibility of utilizing a squirt gun to ward off intruders. I opted for some crafty sarcasm with a newer, not-so polite sign instead:

"Unless you are a Jewish carpenter from Nazareth, please do not disturb us." I thought it was pretty clear but it didn't work any better than my original sign. People popped their heads in to tell me how clever I was.

In desperation, I emailed my friend Deirdre and asked her if she knew where I could rent "a rabid pit bull" to guard my door. When I arrived the next morning, I was greeted by a large, colorful cardboard bulldog with a glowering disposition. Deirdre had named him Fluffy. He was one of those accordion-folded dashboard covers that people use to keep the heat off their steering wheel. We propped him up in the hallway in front of a recycling bin and added a bright orange "SSH TESTING" sign. After that, Fluffy reappeared every time I was proctoring a final exam. He was hard to ignore, and thus was effective at protecting our privacy most of the time.

But not always. At one point, Miss Ingénue stepped over Fluffy to get to my door. "This will just take a minute," she said. It was late in the day and I was tired.

"You need to leave!!!" I barked at her. She turned in a huff and stomped down the stairs. Friends later told me she marched into the teachers' room and told everyone within earshot what a flaming bitch I was. Now *that* was effective. People avoided me like the plague.

Why didn't I do that years ago?

Hospital Road Trip

By the spring of her senior year, Lucretia had already passed all her graduation exams except for one social studies test that was required by the state. She had previously failed it twice. Per her testing modifications, she was entitled to have the test read aloud to her, so to maximize her chances of success, I urged her to plan on doing that. She had been resistant about being read to in the past.

"I wanna take my test with you," Lucretia said.

"I know you do, honey. I wish I could sit with you individually, but I can't. I have six other students that need to take the same exam. I can't read the test to you with them in the room. It violates the integrity of *their* tests if I do that. They aren't allowed readers like you are."

"Well then, why can't they work with someone else?" she asked me.

"Lucretia, how can I ask someone to work with six of my students while I work with only one? I know it sucks. I hate making decisions like this. I got you a really good reader. You know Mr. Peters, the business teacher. You'll like working with him."

"Miss Carroll, no. I'm not going to work with anyone else. I will take it with you and the other kids, and if I have a question, I can call you over and you can explain it to me."

I felt awful. I looked at the names of the other six kids taking the same test at the same time. Yes, Lucretia was entitled to a reader, but she was not my only student. Other kids had the same graduation requirement. One of them had a short fuse and could be explosive when stressed. Another one would shut down and refuse to continue when he was frustrated. I wondered about asking another resource teacher to take on my group of six, but my coworkers were already overloaded. It was a Sophie's choice dilemma.

"OK, I can certainly come over and read a question or two in your ear if you're stuck. You may have to wait a little if I'm busy with someone else."

"That's fine, Miss. We'll make it work."

By the time her testing day arrived, I was more optimistic about Lucretia's chances. She had studied and taken several practice exams, and gone for private tutoring sessions with Mrs. Calhoun, her social studies teacher.

Before I even left for school that morning, I was feeling anxious. A good friend, Mark, was in a local hospital having double-bypass surgery the same day. Mark lived alone. He had fibbed and told the folks at the hospital I was family so I would be allowed in, and left me the phone number of his estranged brother in Manhattan . . . just in case.

Lucretia and her classmates arrived at 12:30 for their afternoon exam and we got started. The test started with 50 multiple-choice questions, and then there were two essays. I read through the directions and the introductions to the essay questions. I reminded them that often there were questions in the first part of the test that contain information related to their essay topics.

For the next several hours, I floated from student to student monitoring their progress. Lucretia was focused and working hard. After a while, several kids were feeling restless, so we decided to take a break. Everyone left their tests on their desks while I locked the door. We all walked to the bathroom in silence, taking the long way back so we could stretch our legs, and then we went back to work. Students started finishing up. I looked over their paperwork and checked the answer sheets to be sure they had signed the *I-did-not-cheat-on-this-test* affidavit on the bottom of the page.

By 4:45, everyone had finished up except for Lucretia. I asked her if there was anything I could help her with.

"Can we start at the beginning?" she asked me.

The beginning, I thought. *Really?*

She had completed most of the questions, but she wanted to double check. She wanted to double check everything.

But it's almost five o'clock. And I still need to go to the hospital to check on Mark.

I swallowed my angst and pulled up a chair. For the next hour and forty-five minutes, I read her every question and every answer choice. I re-read the essay questions and highlighted the specifics of what the two tasks were asking her to write about. She finished at 6:30, and she felt pretty good about it. Nervous, but pretty good.

"Lucretia, do you have a ride coming?" I asked.

Cell phones hadn't been invented yet. "Can I use your phone, Miss?" she asked me. "I will call my mom."

I took her test paperwork with me and went to the bathroom. Breathing a deep sigh of relief, I felt myself starting to relax. Then I went to the main office to check my mail, but it was closed and the lights were off. I wasn't surprised. It was pretty late.

Well, I can lock up her test until tomorrow. That's OK. Not a problem.

I walked back up the stairs to my room and smiled at Lucretia. She was sitting at my desk, putting the headset of the phone back in the cradle.

"There is no answer. She must not be home yet. I can try again in a little while."

"OK, honey," I locked her test in my filing cabinet.

So much for starting to relax. I really have to get out of here. I have to check on Mark.

Lucretia's house was more than two miles from school. Normally she rode public transportation, but neither one of us knew the bus schedule at that time of day. Per school policy, I wasn't supposed to offer her a ride, but how could I leave Lucretia stranded?

A little after seven o'clock, she called her house again.

Come on Mom, pick up the phone. Pick up the phone.

Her mom still wasn't home.

That's it. Screw the "no kids in your car" rule.

"Lucretia, I have a problem. I'll give you a ride home, but I have to go to the hospital first. I have a friend who had major surgery today. I really need to get up to St. Matthew's before eight and check on him. If I take you home first, I won't make it. I'm not going to stay long. Maybe ten minutes, tops."

She smiled at me. "Sure, Miss. I'll go to the hospital."

We piled into my Jeep. "Maybe we can get something to eat in the hospital cafeteria," I told her. Thanks to another *Johnny Quest* map my husband had drawn for me, I managed to find St. Matthew's with no problem. I could not believe my good luck when I found a parking space at a meter right in front of the hospital. I lined up my Jeep with the car in front of the open spot so I could parallel park. I cranked the steering wheel . . . a little too far. I stepped on the gas . . . a little too hard . . . and immediately heard a loud pop.

NO!

"What was that?" Lucretia asked.

"Shit. Shit. Shit." I jumped out of the car and looked at the back tire, which was pressed much too tightly against the curb. "That," I told Lucretia, "Was the sound of a tire going flat."

"Oh, no, Miss!" Lucretia cried to me. "What are we gonna do?"

"We're gonna call my husband," I told her. I opened my wallet to look for some coins.

"Lucretia, do you have any change for the meter? I only have one quarter, and I need that to call John."

Lucretia fed a couple coins to the parking meter and we went into the lobby. After finding a row of payphones, I went back into my wallet and pulled out my last quarter. Blessedly, John answered right away.

"Where are you? Still at the hospital?"

"We just got here. Testing ran late, and Lucretia didn't have a ride home, and I have to get to the ICU before eight. And I just got a flat tire."

And I just want to start screaming, but I have a student with me so I can't.

"How did you do that?" John wondered.

"I ran into the curb. Do you want me to call AAA? Or do you wanna come up here? I really should learn to change a tire myself."

Please come. I am drowning here.

"I can get there faster than they can," he told me. Go check on Mark."

Thanks, buddy.

"I'll have Lucretia call her mom and then go upstairs."

Lucretia interrupted me. "Miss, I don't have any more quarters. And neither do you."

Oh crap.

"John, now I need another favor. Can you call Lucretia's mom and tell her what's going on? I don't want her to wonder where Lucretia is. I don't have any more change for the phone."

"Sure. Put her on."

Lucretia gave John her phone number and her mom's name while I looked for directions to the ICU. Then we found an elevator and meandered through a couple hallways to our destination.

I approached the nurse's station. A nurse in green scrubs looked up from some paperwork and peered at me over top of her glasses.

"Can you help me?" I asked her. "We're looking for Mark Kellerman."

"Are you family?"

"Mark is our uncle. We're his only family in town." I told her. She looked at me with my pale Irish skin and red hair.

Then she looked at Lucretia with her luminous black skin and cornrow braids. Lucretia smiled at her. Broadly.

"He's right over here. You can only stay a minute." She led us to a corner room.

"Yes, of course," I replied. "Did the surgery go well?"

"He did great. He will sleep through the night. He should be awake tomorrow morning if you want to call then. Or you can come back for a brief visit tomorrow afternoon," she suggested, as she pulled back the curtain.

I watched Mark's chest go up. I watched it go down. I listened to the machines beeping and watched the pulsing wave of the heart monitor.

He's OK. Mark is OK. I got here on time and he's OK.

Satisfied that Mark was in good hands, I took a deep breath and turned back to Lucretia. "Ok, honey, we can go."

The cafeteria was closed, so we went outside to wait for John. It was less than fifteen minutes before he arrived.

"Did you talk to Lucretia's mom?" I asked him.

"I did," John answered, as he twisted his 4-way wrench on a lug nut. "She was grateful for the call." He changed the tire in record time and then kissed me goodbye. Lucretia and I piled back into my Jeep and put on our seatbelts. I checked my mirrors before pulling away from the curb.

"Miss, thank you so much for driving me home. I'm glad your friend is OK."

"I'm just glad we got here in time. Glad John got hold of your mom. Everything worked out."

"Yeah, everything . . ." She was silent for a few moments, then Lucretia turned to face me again. "Do you think I passed my test, Miss?"

"I will drop it off to the grading team in the morning. I promise you I will call as soon as I know something."

"OK, but use a code word, Miss. Don't say I passed. Just say oink."

"Oink?"

"Yeah. I'm so nervous. I don't wanna think about pass or fail. Just say oink if I made it."

I smiled at her. "Hokey dokey." I told her. "Oink is the password."

I dropped Lucretia off at her house, and half an hour later I pulled in my own driveway. It was a little before nine p.m. After consuming a very large bowl of peppermint ice cream with hot fudge sauce, I fell in bed.

I dropped Lucretia's test off to the grading team the next morning, and then went back to my room for another round of testing. Blessedly, I only had a couple kids and their exam was not terribly difficult. After a couple hours, they started checking over their answers. Then my phone rang.

I wasn't going to answer it, but my gut told me to pick it up.

"Oink, Oink, Miss Carroll. Oink, Oink, Oink."

"Lucretia?"

"Mrs. Calhoun called me. You remember I went to her for some extra tutoring?"

"Oh my G – You passed it! That is fabulous!"

"I'm so happy." I could almost hear her grinning.

"You should be very proud of yourself," I told her.

"I am. Miss, I wanted to ask you . . . how is your friend Mark?"

"I called the hospital this morning and talked with his nurse. Mark's condition is oink."

True or False

Directions: Determine whether the following statements are true or false.

1. One June, a math Regents exam was so poorly constructed that massive multitudes of students failed the test. Many seniors at Baldwin and elsewhere across the state were in danger of not graduating until the New York State Commissioner of Education relented and threw out the test.

2. According to multiple sources, before I arrived at Baldwin a sports team took part in a theater production and mooned the audience.

3. A Baldwin administrator once sent an email stating: "Just a reminder that Annual Review Packets are due March 26. If you have any question or concerns please contact me. I will be sending this out via e-mail. If you do not receive this please send me your e-mail address."

4. The same administrator once requested information about a child that had been identified as having "Attention Defecate" Disorder.

5. On multiple occasions, Baldwin resource teachers stayed at school until 6:30 pm administering exams during Regents Week.

6. A Baldwin social studies teacher told his class that the horrors of the Holocaust had been grossly exaggerated and some of the events were filmed by Hollywood studios.

7. At a faculty meeting, Principal Len announced that any teacher wishing to request an excused absence to attend a conference would have to make arrangements to have their classes covered by other teachers. The other teachers would have to give up their planning periods to accommodate the request.

8. After much friction with the Board of Education, one of our superintendents left to take a job in another district where he was charged with embezzling thousands of dollars in district funds. He pled guilty to theft and tax fraud and spent 30 days in jail. He died still owing about $300,000 in unpaid taxes and penalties.

9. A Baldwin student entered the women teachers' bathroom once whilst I was seated behind the stall door and said, "Miss Carroll, I need you. I know it's you, I recognize your Birkenstocks."

10. One September, a student came to my door during a second block, said he was joining our resource class, and showed me his schedule. Indeed, it said second block, room 200, but the teacher listed was C. Jackson instead of P. Carroll, and the class listed was Computer Applications 1 instead of Resource. I suggested we go next door to room 202, where the Computer Applications classes were taught. I showed the schedule to Mr. Linden, the teacher, but he had never heard of C. Jackson, and he was teaching Computer Applications 2. I was under the impression that the schedule had the wrong room, the wrong teacher, and the wrong class. It turned out the student was in the wrong high school.

11. A police officer, stationed at Baldwin High School, once asked me if I was aware that I "intimidated some people right down to their shorts."

12. A girl in the hallway outside of English Teacher Joanne's classroom was disrupting her class and spouting all kinds of nonsense. Joanne stepped to the door and told the noisy young woman to move along. Indignant, the girl told her to mind her own business, wherein Joanne responded, "This hallway is my business, bitch."

13. One year, teachers were required to have students complete a "performance task" that was specific to their subject area. The performance task for the Electrical Trades Teachers in our district was to have the kids build circuit breakers . . . as a pretest.

Do you know what can happen when you build a circuit breaker incorrectly? You can get electrocuted.

14. When a young lady at Baldwin took off her earrings and smeared Vaseline on her hair and face, she was mostly likely

planning to start a fight with someone, as Vaseline offered some protection against fingernails and made it difficult to yank hair out by the roots.

15. Peta, an English teacher, attended an annual review of a special education student from one of her inclusion classes. She learned the student was slated to receive a "certificate of attendance" diploma, even after Peta told the committee members that the student had been present in her class twice during the entire semester.

16. A former student stopped by one day after school in a wedding gown to tell me she had just gotten married and to introduce me to her husband.

17. Despite the ominous winter weather forecast one day, a superintendent did *not* cancel school as did his counterparts in neighboring districts. When he finally decided to send us

home at 11 a.m., the roads were already impassable. Some students were stranded at school until 8 p.m. that night.

18. Economics teacher Jack McGill stuffed mailboxes with a memo on April Fool's Day one year. It was printed on district letterhead and gave detailed instructions about a new requirement wherein teachers would be required to punch a time clock every day when they entered and left the building. A time card was attached to the memo. Mass pandemonium ensued, and the union phone lines blew up before Mr. McGill fessed up.

19. During a budget crisis, teachers were restricted in the number of copies they could request for their class assignments. Teachers were given vouchers, referred to as "Baldwin Money" at the beginning of each month which they would use to "buy" copies when they needed them. This

strategy was ultimately ineffective because teachers coped by making copies of the Baldwin money.

20. My teammate Chuck was starting a unit on Japan in his 9th grade social studies class and asked his students if anyone knew what an archipelago was. He was confused when one young man answered that an archipelago was "like the father on the Brady Bunch."

Answer Key: All answers are true. I'm clever, but I couldn't make this stuff up. I witnessed most of them myself. Others were relayed to me by people I trust implicitly. And if you were confused like Chuck was in the last question, it's because Mr. Brady was an archi*tect*, not an archi*pelago*.

Boiled Frog

Maureen McGuire graduated. . . . oh, I lose track of time. In the late 80s? Her dad told a great story about how we adapt to changing circumstances. We adapt and adapt and sometimes we adapt ourselves to death without even realizing it. Dad's story is about a frog in a pot of water. You drop him in a big vat of boiling water and he screams, "NO! I may be a frog, and I may love the water, but I ain't doing this." He leaps out immediately to save himself from impending doom.

Then you take the same frog and put him in another pot of water, except this time the water is a nice comfortable temperature. After a bit, you turn the heat up just a few degrees. Froggy notices the change in temperature, but much like that first plunge into the ocean on a beach vacation, he adjusts after a few minutes. He is perhaps not quite as comfortable as he was before, but he adapts and carries on. Time passes and the heat is turned up again, and he continues to acclimate to the change. The process continues. The heat keeps rising. And before he understands what has happened, Kermit has boiled to death.

At Baldwin, we were beginning to feel a similar heat. After multiple visits from various groups of suits, and lots of number crunching, we had been identified as a "Persistently Low Achieving (PLA)" school by the New York State Education Department. There are a couple ways this can happen. In Baldwin's case, it was because graduation scores had dropped to less than 60 % for three consecutive years. The reasons *why* the scores were low did not matter. When a school is designated PLA, the New York State Government steps in, and the school district under review has a few different choices as to how to proceed. None of the choices are painless.

Our superintendent and board of education decided to choose the *transformational model* for our district because it was deemed the least disruptive. Under this plan, a PLA school has their own redesign team, composed of teachers and administrators. The principal of each affected school is typically replaced, along with some of the staff. The New York State Ed department provides "Annual Professional Performance Review Data." This information, combined with teacher evaluations written by administrators, is used to remove ineffective teachers. There is an increase in both students' instructional time and teachers' collaboration time. Statistics are constantly reviewed to improve instruction.

Because multiple schools in Baldwin's district became PLA at about the same time, a large number of teachers would be transferred out of one school and into another school simultaneously. That was a whole lot of shuffling of employees. My husband suggested we drive to the front lawns of each school, remove the name signs out front, and switch them with the signs from the other schools. Presto Chango - this is now a new school with a new staff. I thought that was a great idea.

Instead, teachers had to reapply to keep their jobs. There was an "interview" process, which consisted of our writing a one-paragraph response about what we had to offer a new and improved Baldwin. After that, groups of us met with members of the redesign team and got more information that detailed what our new school plan would look like. Ninety-five percent daily attendance from staff was expected. There would be mandatory (paid) professional development for a week in the summer, and twice a week after school all year long. Staff attendance at five after-school events was required.

Depending on scheduling needs, some teachers would be required to teach an additional class for additional pay, rather than have a duty period. New York State would infuse the district with a whole lot of money to help pay for these changes. Baldwin's redesign team would ultimately determine which educators would stay and which ones would transfer to other buildings.

In typical district office manner, the exiting Baldwin teachers found out they *weren't* coming back in the worst possible way. Principal Len's plan was to speak with people privately. Unfortunately, Len was out of the building when somebody at the district office decided that teachers would be notified ahead of schedule. An administrative intern showed up at teachers' doors with transfer letters in hand. Hysteria ensued. I learned that I was staying put when I did not get a letter.

Prior to this, I had asked a member of the redesign team if there were any surprises about who was coming back and who wasn't. She said there were a few. Indeed, she was right. There were some ineffective people who were moved, but at

Baldwin, and across the district, there were also teachers with very good records who had been moved around. Teachers with many, many years of experience who were, in my opinion, being invited to retire because of their bigger paychecks.

The summer professional development was a terrific waste of time. In the summer of 2011, we got paid $37 an hour for 20 hours of work over five days. We were supposed to be there from 9 a.m. - 1 p.m. but most days we left early. One day we left at 11. Do the math folks. One hundred teachers times 20 hours times $37 an hour is $74,000 for *one* school.

We were given two texts to read that were to become our Bible/Koran/Torah for the next three years. One of them was guaranteed to cure all the ills of education. It said so, right in the first chapter. If you didn't see success, it's because you implemented it wrong. It said that in the first chapter, too. The two soft cover books cost. . . I don't know, maybe $20 apiece . . . there's another $4000 dollars. Plus the trainer's salary. There was nothing wrong with her teaching strategies, but after a lifetime in the classroom, none of it was groundbreaking new information. Cooperative groups. Word walls. Venn Diagrams. Vocabulary builders. Bubble Maps. Gallery Walks. Additionally, the trainer spent an inordinate amount of time discussing yet *another new-and-improved* lesson plan format. If we could just write good lesson plans, our scores would improve. Kids would graduate. Global warming would disappear and we would all join hands and sing Kumbaya.

The special ed administrator in my building said our resource students would be grouped by "similarity of individual needs", which was interpreted to mean the same grade level. No longer would we get kids in 9th grade and follow them through to graduation. The relationships we had developed with existing students and their parents would be severed.

New interim assessments would be required for all students. Kids would periodically be evaluated in each of the core areas (English, math, science, social studies) that were paired with an eventual Regents graduation exam. The practice tests would be written ahead of time. They would be posted online for all teachers to read. Subject area teachers would study the test. They would bond with the tests. They would teach to the tests.

Is it getting hot in here, or is it just me?

Test results would be analyzed, question by question. Graphs and grids would be filled out. How many students missed question #6? Let the re-teaching begin! In addition to moving forward with the rest of the class, now teachers will somehow carve out time to work with a small group of students who need reinforcement on specific concepts.

At a faculty meeting one day, a teacher said, "That may be difficult. I have two students who have shown up only twice since the semester started. One of them is busy with his private pharmaceutical business on the corner, and the other one had to watch his younger siblings because mom's work shift changed."

Quoting New York State regulations, Principal Len answered, "Your evaluation will now be based in part on how many of your students are successful. Numbers will be tallied. Percentages will be figured. Teachers who do not meet the bar will be transferred or terminated."

Another teacher said, "Len, I love working with my special needs students, but due to their learning disabilities, many of them will have great difficulty getting through the Regents exam for this class. Other teachers have all college prep classes. Those students will likely do better on the exams. Surely it is not appropriate to hold us to the same standard."

Principal Len once again answered; "Your evaluation will now be based in part on how many of your students are successful. Numbers will be tallied. Percentages will be figured. Teachers who do not meet the bar will be transferred or terminated."

Yet another teacher said, "There are so many pieces to this problem that we cannot control. We have students who are homeless, who have parents in jail, who have lost loved ones to gun violence, who are gang members, who don't know if they are going to eat dinner tonight. School is not number one on their agenda."

Principal Len repeated himself once more; "Your evaluation will now be based in part on how many of your students are successful. Numbers will be tallied. Percentages will be figured. Teachers who do not meet the bar will be transferred or terminated."

Somebody open a window please. Or turn on the fan.

I went to see a former principal who took a new job as the director of high schools. He had always been supportive of me and was a good counsel. After many years in the biz, I wanted a job description because I was being pulled in so many different directions. The special ed administrator in my building said resource teachers would be required to teach lessons that would directly relate to the new assessments. The director of special ed downtown wanted us to work on IEP goals. The kids wanted help with their daily work. Classroom teachers wanted kids to use resource time to finish a test, or make up a lab the kids missed.

Is the air conditioning broken?

I was hoping Director of High Schools Brad, aka my former principal Brad, could give me some guidance. Was I supposed to do what I had always done and teach compensation strategies? Re-teach a difficult concept the kids had learned in the classroom? Help them with their challenging projects? Provide testing accommodations? Network with staff and parents? Help students work through behavior issues? Give them access to recorded books and technology?

Brad said he would look into it for me. He would ask Special Ed Director Bart . . . no, wait, that wouldn't work. Bart had such a humongous ego. He would ask Assistant Director Luella to speak to Special Ed Director Bart, and let him think providing a job description was *his* idea . . . yeah, that would work. He would get back to me. So I waited a week. Then two. And I emailed Director of High Schools Brad, who said *yes, he had asked* for clarification about the specific duties of a resource teacher. First from Assistant Director Luella, and then from Special Ed Director Bart. They laughed in his face. Both of them.

I closed out Brad's email, more confused than ever. I was living in Bizarro World. Up was down, and down was up. I didn't know how to proceed. I knew one thing, though. Trouble was coming.

There goes the thermostat again. Damn it's getting hot in here.

Bits and Pieces

Mr. Know-it-all

Nobody called Mr. Know-it-all by his real name. Not the kids, and not his coworkers. He was a comical sight in his forest-green polyester suit. It was so tight his tushie peeked out the back slit of his jacket, and he always wore that suit with a loud mismatched tie. Those of us with more experience used to try to avoid him. I would duck into the ladies' room when I saw him coming. His intrusive behavior was frequently a hot topic for the Baldwin gossip mill.

Know-it-all was a technology teacher at Baldwin when I first arrived, and he made an instant impression on me because of the way he alienated people. Like Henny Penny, he loved to spread doom and gloom.

"You went to Vassar," he once told my friend Joanne. "What are you doing, wasting your life here? Your parents didn't spend good money for your education so you could work in this hell hole. *These* kids are animals. Their *parents* are animals. Don't bother trying to actually *teach* them anything."

The sun rose and set according to Mr. Know-it-all. He not only knew all there was to know on every subject imaginable; it was his burden in life to be sure you knew it too. He scurried around the building, positioning himself in stairwells, furtively looking around corners while he hunted his unsuspecting prey. I was not always successful at escaping his snare.

"Have you heard about this new reading program the district wants to try?" he snarled. "It's a waste of time. It will never work."

"Well, how do you know? We haven't even tried it yet."

"Those programs *never* work. I have seen it all before."

His favorite victims were the student teachers. Sometimes one of them would exit the teachers' room, turn a corner, and Know-it-all would pounce:

"You're new here, aren't you?"

"Yes, I'm Brighteye Bushytail. I'm doing my student teaching."

"You should get out of education while you still have time."

"Excuse me?"

"You know it's a waste of energy. Administrators have all the power. You can't change anything. We are just pawns in their game. You can't possibly make a difference."

"I don't believe that."

"Oh, no, no, no! I am a career educator. I have years of experience. I have a master's degree. You need to listen to me. This place is going to hell in a hand basket."

We were constantly amazed at Know-it-all's ability to be outrageous. I often thought that after he left teaching, Know-it-all would enjoy working for "The Smoking Gun" or one of those conspiracy theory websites. Do research on the aliens at Roswell. Unravel the JFK mystery. Find out what really happened to Biggie and Tupac and Elvis. He would have been right at home.

Class Roster

Our teaching team met once a week to discuss common concerns and eat fabulous fattening snacks that we would take turns bringing in from home. There were always schedule changes at the beginning of the year, but one particular September, Social Studies Teacher Chuck Green firmly stated he would not accept any more "T" students in his third-block class. Normally Chuck was a very Zen guy, so I was surprised by his pronouncement.

"Chuck, what are you talking about?" I asked him.

Instead of answering me, he pulled out his attendance book and opened it up.

"Look at this," he said, pointing to the page with his right index finger. I leaned in to look. "They're nice kids, but how am I going to learn all their names?"

My eyes scanned the page . . . Chuck Green, US History, Block 3, I moved to the roster of names . . . and then I saw it. Theresa, Tara, Tad, Takisha, Timothy, Titus, Tristan, Thomas, Talia, Talesha, Tabitha, Tobias, Terry, Tashondra, Tammy, Tito, Tony, Terrance, Tali, Trevor, Tristan, . . . I couldn't help myself. I started giggling. My eyes moved farther down the list.

"Oh, look, Chuck, here's a Mary."

"Not anymore," he smirked. "The other kids told me she moved over the summer."

Mr. Rat

After Joanne and I stepped away from supervising school shows, Glen Howard became the new director. He taught English and Theater Arts in the old chorus room, where the seating was elevated in tiers, and arranged in the three quarter round. The furniture included desks, tables, stuffed chairs, and several odd couches that periodically made their way onto the stage. The couches were pushed up against the back wall, on the top tier. One day Glen was absent from school.

The substitute teacher was taking attendance that day when a bonafide rat, no doubt uncomfortable with the pressing weight of the students seated on the couch cushions above him, crawled out from underneath the pillows and scurried across the floor. The sub started screaming. Several burly football players joined in the chorus and then sought higher ground on top of available tables in the classroom. One of them picked up a chair.

Perhaps he should have given up football and taken up pitching baseballs, because the chair he heaved across the room hit Mr. Rat and stunned him pretty good. The student continued his assault on the rodent by reenacting a clogging scene from *Riverdance*, and stomped Mr. Rat to death, to the great relief of his classmates.

Glen's kids couldn't wait to tell him about it when he returned to class, and he couldn't wait to share it with the rest of the faculty. We all laughed about it for a couple weeks.

A few months later, I was surfing the web when I came upon a stuffed rat, available from Gund Company, makers of wonderfully detailed toys. I gave in to temptation and ordered one for Glen. I had one of my students deliver said creature to his room the day before Christmas break. Upon opening the package, Glen gathered some safety pins and affixed the beastie to his left shoulder, looking rather like a pirate with a pet parrot. During his planning time that day, he strutted upstairs and knocked at my door.

"Aaaargh," he sneered when I opened the door. "Ave ye met me new shipmate? This be Mr. Rat."

I started to cackle as he continued. "He's right handy fer keeping the scalawags in line." Glen noticed the students in my room, trying to finish up an assignment before the Christmas break. "I see ye are still toiling in the labors of the day, so I will nah tarry any longer. Ye 'ave yerself a bonny holiday, lassie."

With that, he turned and dragged his imaginary peg leg down the hallway.

Dominique

Have you ever heard of amelia? I don't mean Amelia Earhart, the missing pilot, or Amelia Bedilia, the title character from Peggy Parrish's kids' books. I mean the medical condition. It comes from the Greek, meaning, "a lack of," and it refers to a congenital absence of one of more limbs of the body.

You may remember the stories of the babies in the 1960s whose mothers were given the drug thalidomide, or the children of Vietnam vets who had been exposed to Agent Orange, or the Russian children whose pregnant moms lived near Chernobyl when the nuclear reactors dumped radiation into the environment. Sometimes the cause of amelia is known, and sometimes it is not. Something happens when the fetus is in the early stages of development, and a baby is born without a limb.

Dominique was one of Theresa's resource students. She was bright and funny young woman who had shortened arms with no elbows. She had fully functional wrists, hands and fingers at the end of her arms, but her arms themselves were the length of a three-quarter sleeve top. When I first met her I did a double take because Dominique was writing an essay at the time. Her handwriting was impeccable. She had no issues at all with manipulating a pen or pencil, or the computer keyboard, or dressing herself, or brushing her hair or her teeth, or any of the million things we do with our hands and fingers every single day. I actually wondered why she even *had* a resource teacher, but I didn't know all the particulars. Maybe she had a learning disability I was unaware of.

Theresa had asked me to cover a class one day because she had to run to a meeting for a few minutes. I started to ask Dominique if she needed help with something, but I could see she was doing just fine on her own. I loved this girl's attitude. She was independent and enthusiastic and delightful. As it turned out, she could also be a little imp.

Springtime at Baldwin and warm weather brought out the short shorts and the miniskirts. One year my student Kiki and I stood in my doorway during passing time and watched the parade of young ladies go by. School policy mandated that shorts had to be fingertip length, meaning that when you extended your arms and put your hands down, your shorts had to be as long as your fingertips. Most of the students complied, but there were always a few girls that wore Daisy

Dukes that were so short that their butt cheeks hung out. At one point, Kiki started scoring the offenders by holding up index cards with numbers on them, channeling Len Goodman from *Dancing with the Stars*.

"Oooh, that's a nine," she would say.

Each year, an administrator got on the intercom and reminded Baldwinites that appropriate attire must be worn at all times. Any student who wore ultra-short clothing would be sent home to change. Every year the announcement was repeated, and every year we had students who pushed the envelope.

Dominique was one of the "pushees." She was in the entry area of the building chatting with friends when Administrator Jamila approached her. I heard the story from Jamila later that day.

"Young lady, your shorts are too short. You know we have a rule about that. Your shorts must be fingertip length."

"But they *are,*" said Dominique. She laid her hands by her sides. As her fingertips reached the edge of her shorts, Dominique coyly smiled.

"Well," said Jamila, shaking her head. "You've got me there."

Lee

Lee had dreamed of being a fireman since he was a little boy. When he was a teenager, he had been in the Firemen's Explorers Program. Lee was hardworking, polite, and often very funny. He was also a concrete thinker. He viewed issues in crystal clear terms of black and white, and there was never any wiggle room for discussion. Lee was in Chuck Green's Social Studies class one day when Chuck was talking about the complex issue of undocumented immigrants crossing into the United States from Mexico. Chuck asked the class if they had any ideas about how to deal with this difficult problem. Lee raised his hand.

"It's easy, Mr. Green," Lee said. "First you get a whole bunch of guards with assault rifles. Then you line them up on our side of the border, every ten feet or so, and when someone illegally enters the country, you shoot 'em down dead. Then you leave the bodies there to discourage other illegal immigrants."

When I heard this story from Chuck, I was horrified. I broached the subject with Lee the next time I saw him. Lee was respectful of me, but he was resolute. A rule was a rule. Anyone who broke the law had to suffer the consequences. Trying to discuss it with him was like debating with a reinforced steel door, so I suggested that he and I "agree to disagree." Lee then asked me for some help with an assignment and we let the issue drop. But our debate game was destined to repeat itself:

"Miss Carroll, I think anyone who skips class should be barred from graduation."

"Sounds a little harsh to me, Lee," I answered.

"Oh, I don't mean they don't graduate. They would still get their diploma. They just can't participate in the ceremony."

"Still seems a little harsh."

"But it's disrespectful to skip class. They shouldn't get to walk the stage. They shouldn't have that privilege," he continued.

"Lee, first of all, that would eliminate a whole lot of students. Secondly, graduation is a milestone. It's a family celebration. Banning students for such a minor offense would also deprive their moms and dads from experiencing the event. That would be a huge loss for those families."

"Well, those kids should think about that before they skip a class," he countered.

Lee had dug in. I was not going to change his mind, and as much as I disagreed with him, he was entitled to his opinion. I needed to redirect him to his assignment, so I smiled like a Cheshire cat and lied through my teeth:

"You're right, Lee." That ended the conversation.

This discussion repeated itself periodically, with topical variations:

"Miss Carroll, don't you think cloning should be illegal?"

"You're right, Lee."

"Miss Carroll, I think we should blow Saddam Hussein off the face of the earth."

"You're right, Lee."

"Gay marriage should be illegal."

"You're right, Lee."

It wasn't long before Lee caught on.

"Miss Carroll, are you just agreeing with me to shut me up?"

"You're right, Lee."

When he could no longer debate a hot topic with me, he moved on to his classmates. Having overheard my response several times, they followed my lead and just agreed with him. Finally I hung a "You're right, Lee" sign on the bulletin board that we could point to when the need arose.

A couple years after he graduated, he called the main office, and a secretary transferred the call to my room. Lee had put his dream of becoming a fireman on the back burner because of a hiring freeze, but finally his acceptance letter to the Firemen's Academy had arrived in the mail.

"It has been *two years*. I finally got in. This is unbelievable." he said to me.

"Lee, "I answered, "You worked hard to follow your dream, and you succeeded. I am *so* proud of you. You should be proud of yourself."

"Yeah. I did." I could picture Lee beaming at me as he spoke. "You're right, Miss."

Briana

I loved Briana to pieces. School was not easy for her, but she worked so hard at it and she always came into my room with a big smile and a positive attitude. Her mom and dad were delightful people and very invested in her education. Briana really surprised me the day she came to school in a short skirt. Really short. If she were to sit down, there would be no fabric between the back of her thighs and the chair. The black spandex was so tight that the outline of her thong underwear was readily apparent. On top of that, her ample cleavage was popping out of a bright orange halter top. She looked like she was ready to film a porno Halloween movie. As she entered my room I said, "No."

"No, what, Miss Carroll?" she asked me.

"No, you are not wearing *that* in my classroom. Call your mother. You are going home to change."

"What's wrong with it?" she purred.

"There's nothing wrong with it," said Nazir, a healthy teenage boy, whose tongue, at that moment, was lapping the floor.

"Call your mother." I gave her the teacher glare. She harrumphed, but she picked up the phone on my desk and called. She left for the office to sign out of the building. It was then that it occurred to me that I probably should have checked this out with an administrator. *Oh well.*

"Miss Carroll, you are no fun" said Nazir.

Briana returned to class about twenty minutes later, wearing a pair of blue jeans, a tee shirt, and a jean jacket.

"What did your mother say?' I asked her.

"My *father* picked me up, and he said if I ever come to school dressed like that again, I will be grounded until I am thirty."

"I didn't think anyone saw you leave the house this morning," I replied.

Apparently, Briana forgave me for sending her home that day. When she graduated she gave me a thank you note that included a little roll of Life Savers candies attached to an index card. On it, she had written, "Just think of yourself as a lifesaver." I still have it hanging on the filing cabinet by my desk.

Evaluation Day

During my time at Baldwin, each student had to meet many requirements to graduate from high school. It reminded me of those outdated Chinese-American restaurant menus that told you to pick "one item from column A and two items from column B," only it was more complex. Twenty-two course credits were mandatory. Four years of English. Four years of social studies. Two years of math. Three years of science. A year of health. Four years of phys. ed. A year of art or music. A multi credit sequence of choice . . . it could be in a foreign language or a vocational strand. A few elective classes.

In addition to the courses, New York State required Regents exams: one in math, one in science, one in English, and two in social studies. 65 was a passing score. Years ago, if *any* student failed a particular Regents exam, he could use a Regents exam variance score - by earning a grade that fell between 55-64 - or by substituting a passing score of 65 on a less rigorous Regents Competency Test. In either of those cases, the student would earn a local diploma instead of a Regents diploma. It might not look as good on an application, but it would help him get accepted to many colleges. Between the required courses and the required exams, the route to graduation was an arduous obstacle course.

Then educational reform reared its head and it got even *more* complicated. *All* students in New York State would earn Regents diplomas. Typical students would have to earn a passing score of 65 on all of their Regents exams.

Kids with disabilities could still pass with a variance Regents exam score of 55-64. Other changes would take place over a number of years. While these requirements were being phased in, kids with learning disabilities would first take the Regents exams. If they were unsuccessful in passing a particular Regents exam, or in earning a variance score, they could continue to substitute a passing score on a Regents Competency Test (RCT) and still graduate with a local diploma. It was referred to as the "The RCT Safety Net." I had the mistaken idea that if the New York State Education Department had authorized it, the safety net was sanctioned. Yes and no.

On the one hand, kids with disabilities could use the Regents exam variance score of 55-64 or the safety net to meet graduation requirements. On the other hand, schools that used either option for graduation would be penalized with a lower score on their New York State Report Card. And Baldwin didn't need any more low marks from the state.

Now kids who had already qualified for graduation were being asked to come back and take exams they didn't need to relieve the pressure being exerted by the state education department.

Yes, you heard that right. Let it sink in for a minute.

New York State regulations required that resource students be grouped by "similarity of individual needs." At Baldwin, this was now interpreted to mean students in the same grade level. First period might be tenth graders. Second period might be eleventh graders. What if a kid can't schedule resource because he is in the wrong section? Guess he will have to drop that photography class he wanted. Instead of working with kids we had been building relationships with since they were ninth graders, resource teachers would trade kids with each other so classes could be arranged by grade level. Perhaps the tradeoff would be worth if kids in the same grade level actual had a "similarity of individual needs." Sadly, that was rarely the case.

Two different tenth graders could have very different needs and different schedules. For math, some took algebra, and others took geometry. In science, it could be either earth science or living environment. A social studies class could be Global Studies I or Global Studies II. That didn't matter, though. As long as you were a 10th grader, you could be assigned to a resource class with any other 10th grader, regardless of what classes you were taking. My head was spinning like the tea cup ride at the state fair.

To prepare those "similarity of individual needs" kids for the Regents exams, we were now required to use resource time to prepare kids for those tests (that some of them didn't even need to take.)

Vance, one of my seniors, had passed four of the five Regents exams, failing only the Global Studies Regents. He was all set to graduate, as he had passed the less demanding Global Studies Regents Competency Test (RCT), but it *made sense* for him to come back and try the Global Studies Regents again. If he passed that last Regents exam, he could receive a Regents diploma.

Tammy, however, had passed *none* of the Regents exams. She had gotten through three RCTs after multiple attempts, and had two more to go. Why would I demand she come back and take Regents exams that were quite obviously a waste of her time? A guidance counselor told me that administrators *really wanted* those kids to retake the exams.

I was not in the mood for this nonsense. "What are they gonna do, Paul? Withhold their diplomas?"

"Well, no, they can't do *that*," he responded.

"Exactly." I said.

In the spring of 2011, Baldwin's Special Ed administrator, Miss Lucy, was scheduling her yearly teacher observations. Rumor had it Lucy was looking for resource teachers to push the "document-based questions (DBQs)" found on both the Global Studies and US History Regents exams. Some of my coworkers pondered putting on a dog and pony show so Lucy could see what she wanted to see. *It's observation day, kiddies. Let's work on a skill you might have no need for to make me look good.*

On the day of my observation, sophomore Tim had a humongous English paper hanging over his head. Because of a couple of school field trips, he was the only student I had that period. It was a rare opportunity for him to have my undivided attention and pound out a lot of work on his paper, which was due the next day. I just couldn't stomach the thought of forcing Tim to work on a practice Global Studies essay when I knew, I *knew*, he was doing well in that class. I had seen some of the compositions he had written. I had networked with Tim's Global Studies teacher. I *knew* he would pass the upcoming regents.

Tim spent the period working on his English paper. We talked about paraphrasing vocabulary and sentence structure. He created a works cited page and I helped him proofread for errors. It was a good lesson, but I wasn't all that surprised when Miss Lucy ripped into me in the post-observation conference.

"Pam, I'm a little concerned. Tim has a Global Studies Regents to take in a few months. Those document-based questions are big points on that test, and you didn't do any prep with him."

"No, not that day, we didn't. Tim is doing really well in his social studies class. His English paper was due the day after my observation, so we worked on that."

My explanation made no difference to her. She prattled on for a while about the importance of the document-based questions. I told her to do whatever she had to do regarding my observation, and I left.

Okay, so I asked for it. I get that, but my bullshit tolerance level had been exceeded. This camel could not carry one more straw. When her evaluation arrived in my mailbox, I was surprised it wasn't worse. It was full of phrases like "it is imperative that Mrs. Carroll provide target instruction" and "it is crucial to prepare students for exams" and went on to push the DBQ practice. To be fair, Lucy *did* find some nice things to say about my relationships with my students. She suggested I continue to work with content area teachers to become familiar with new "benchmark assessments." There was a zinger in her write up about my attendance. I signed the thing and gave it back to her. I went to see my union representative, who freely told me that many of my coworkers also had problems with Miss Lucy. She reminded me that teachers have the option to write a rebuttal if they are unhappy with an observation. I wrote mine the day after Tim got a 79 on his Global Studies regents:

I've been thinking about responding to this evaluation since my post-observation conference, but I decided to wait until Regents test scores came in. In that meeting, the evaluator was critical of the fact that I had not spent time reviewing for the Global Regents exam with one of my students. T.S. took that exam a few days ago, and he earned a score of 79. A resource teacher has many classroom jobs to juggle in addition to preparation for Regents exams: assisting kids with difficult homework assignments, helping with computer research, teaching compensatory skills, counseling students with behavioral issues, and in some cases, RCT prep - for at least the next four years, or until the state extends the safety net again. Apparently not working on Regents review on the particular day of my observation did not cause T.S. to fail his Regents exam.

There were several positive recommendations in my evaluation report about a) becoming familiar with content area curricula and assessments, b) collaborating with subject area teachers, and c) participating in opportunities for staff development. Anyone who knows me knows that I have always done these things, so I find it odd that the evaluator felt a need to address them. Still, I readily agree that they are all good ideas.

Of greater concern to me, however, is the fact that under the heading of "Professional Qualities," the evaluator addressed the fact that I have used fifteen sick days this year. It is true that I have missed more school than I would have liked to. My husband had knee surgery (again), and I wrestled with sciatica for a good part of the school year. I was under the treatment of a specialist and had two appointments for nerve blocks. There were several days I came in when I probably should have stayed home. Further, I received a summons for six weeks of grand jury duty, which I postponed until my upcoming summer vacation so I would not have to spend more time away from the kids. None of my administrators asked me about my attendance. No one made a comment that I was missing too many days. If I had been asked why I had been out, I would have answered honestly. The evaluator instead chose to put it in my formal evaluation under the heading of "Professional Qualities," which I infer to mean that I am somehow not professional.

This is the end of my 27th year in the XXX School District. I have never before received an evaluation that I was less than proud of. Given my history, I believe this evaluation says more about the evaluator than it does about me.

Principal Len was not very happy with Miss Lucy. He reassigned me to another administrator for future evaluations, and I was grateful for that. For three decades in teaching, I had adapted to change and moved forward, but this time things were different. The cumulative stress of many years in urban education was bearing down on me like a freight train named the Rubicon Express.

Darryl

Lots of teachers think they don't get enough recognition for their work. We all get caught up in the day to day activities of our lives. Our administrators get busy with phones ringing or board meetings or conferences or kids smoking in the parking lot or breaking up a fight or curriculum development or the PTSO or chaperoning a basketball game. They direct their energy to whatever plate needs spinning at any given moment, and they don't hand out as many "atta boys" as they should. Not that anyone can really blame them. Some days they don't have enough time to cover the bare essentials. Finding time to compliment their staff becomes a luxury.

Maybe that's one reason it is so gratifying to hear nice things from the kids. "Miss, you've done so much for me. I wouldn't be here it wasn't for you. I really want to thank you." My answer is always the same. If you want to thank me, walk the stage. Graduate. That's all I need.

Darryl came to me as a 5th year senior. He hadn't finished all his graduation requirements in four years. As a student identified with a learning disability, he had the option to stay in school until he was 21. Darryl had transferred to Baldwin from the Detroit area. He was in an inclusion class there, where he spent part of his day in class with a special education teacher, and the rest of his day mainstreamed into academic classes.

I was originally surprised to see Darryl on my class list, as inclusion is typically for kids that need more academic support than resource kids. Some inclusion kids get regular high school diplomas, but many don't. Individual Education Plan (IEP) diplomas are awarded to those special education students who have limited academic abilities and are just not capable of earning a regular diploma. An IEP diploma won't get you into a community college, but it recognizes your efforts in high school. It allows you to participate in the graduation ceremony. After reviewing Darryl's record and talking with his previous guidance counselor in Detroit, I realized he could earn a regular (called a local) diploma by the end of the school year. I knew it would be difficult, but it was, in theory, possible. Darryl had wonderful manners, and a sweet disposition.

Physically, he looked like . . . hmm . . . have you seen that really old Jane Fonda movie, "Cat Ballou?" Stubby Kaye and Nat King Cole were the balladeers in the film, and if you mixed up their DNA together in a Petri dish, that would be Darryl. Not very tall, kind of roly-poly, always smiling, and a melodic tenor voice. Cute. Charming. But with some bad school habits. I really wanted to see him do well.

Darryl's mom, Valene, was his champion. She was a working single mom with a lot of responsibilities. Throughout the school year, I periodically met with her about missing homework, incomplete assignments, and skipped classes. In the spring, I met with her again. Darryl's graduation was in jeopardy because he was failing phys. ed. and biology. Valene was a petite woman, and soft spoken like her son. After listening to my concerns, she spoke to Darryl in her little voice.

"I raised you by myself. I did the best I could. Your graduation is not just about you. It's about your family. It's about me. If you didn't have the ability, that would be one thing. But you do. And if you don't do what you need to do, I guess I'll just throw up my hands and say 'Oh, well.'"

I couldn't see what Darryl was doing at that point because I was hanging my own head and staring at my Birkenstocks. When I picked it up again, I saw that he had turned to a puddle of goo underneath the conference table. Valene's words apparently made an impact, because after that Darryl went to class. He did his homework. He stayed after school to get those biology labs done.

At the very end, everything hinged on one exam. A social studies final, which he needed to pass to graduate, was on Thursday morning. Graduation was Saturday night. He finished his test and I told him I would call him with the results. I took his test into Betty Stevens' room where the social studies department was grading a mountain of exams, with an ocean of essays. They had been at it for days, and they were plenty tired. It really was pretty nervy of me, but I asked Betty to stop what she was doing and grade Darryl's test immediately. She knew Darryl, she knew the stakes, and she took the exam. I pretended to do a Sudoku puzzle while she graded it. She told me the results.

I walked out of her room in a daze. I started down the stairs as tears were welling in my eyes. I walked into Tawanda, now a senior and a classmate of Darryl's, and her mom. They had stopped in to pick up tickets for the graduation ceremony. Tawanda saw my face, put her arm around my shoulder, concerned, and asked, "What's wrong?"

I found my breath and choked out the words. "Nothing's wrong. Darryl graduates." Tawanda threw her arms around me and held me as the tears fell.

That, my friends, is why teachers teach. For those victories. In a thirty year career, you will get a few of them, if you're lucky. They are the moments that sustain us through the stress and the disappointments and the bullshit that is inherent in this profession. These are the moments that put gas in our gas tank and help us get back in the car and keep chugging down the road.

Graduation time. Darryl's name was read. He stepped across the stage. He shook the principal's hand. He greeted a few members of the board of education who had come to the commencement ceremony. After the final handshake, Darryl held his diploma in both hands over top of his head. He turned to the crowd and loudly said, "I did it, Mama." I would have started bawling again, but at that precise moment, his mortarboard fell off his head. Laughing with the rest of us, he scrambled to pick it up, walked off the stage, and into his future.

Cabana Boy

I had a policy of not attending graduation parties. I believed if I accepted one invitation, I had to accept all of them. The year I directed my first musical, with its massive cast, I was probably invited to 15 or 20 get-togethers, all of which were scheduled for the same weekend. It was just easier to tell the kids I couldn't go.

Several years after that, Peter became my student. He was a kind-hearted, respectful young man who had a problem with procrastination and follow through. He had a tough time navigating his way through high school. His mom and I talked frequently to monitor his progress, and happily, in the end, he pulled it off and graduated from Baldwin. Peter's celebration was being held at a lakeside summer family home on a gorgeous Sunday afternoon. It was the only graduation party I had been asked to attend that year, so I broke my own rule and decided to go. John tagged along. He wore a Hawaiian shirt and a pair of jeans.

I had barely gotten out of the car when the accolades started. The first person I saw was Peter's brother Noah, whom I had met a couple times at school events.

"Miss Carroll! Oh My God! Miss Carroll is here," Noah shrieked. He swung open the screen door to the cottage and ran inside. John got out of the car.

"Is that Peter?" John asked me.

"That's his younger brother," I answered. People were milling around the yard. There was a group sitting at one of the picnic tables, and another group playing bocce ball on the lawn. John and I went inside the front door.

"Miss Carroll, Oh, I am so glad you came," said Mrs. Charleston, Peter's mom, embracing me. "Peter has been telling all his relatives about you. He will be thrilled to see you."

"We're glad to come. Your home is lovely." I rested my hand on John's back and introduced him. "This is John, my husband." As John shook Mrs. Charleston's hand, Peter appeared. He barreled into me with a big bear hug.

"Hi, Miss! You came!" He took my hand and dragged me across the room. "Come meet my grandmother."

I met Grandma. And Cousin Billy. And Uncle Alan and Aunt Maude, and their three daughters. I met the neighbors, the Hoffmanns, and their two border collies Buster and Miriam. I met Peter's godparents, Jack and Gloria Brayton. I spent the afternoon being passed from one party goer to another, all of whom wanted to hug me and thank me for "all I had done for Peter." I won't lie . . . I loved it.

The hamburgers were coming off the grill and people were lining up at the buffet table. I sheepishly realized I hadn't seen John in quite some time. Remembering that he had worn a Hawaiian shirt, I used my teacher voice and asked no one in particular, "Has anyone seen my cabana boy?"

A gentleman scooping macaroni salad onto his plate pointed to one of the picnic tables.

"He's holding a place for you over there," he answered.

Indeed, John was patiently waiting for me, chatting with another guest and making himself to home. When he saw me looking in his direction, he smiled and pointed to the empty seat next to him. I walked over with my plate and sat down.

"How's the food?" I asked him.

"Did you get some of the potato salad? It's really good."

As I sat there, watching him happily dive into his plate, I felt a familiar warmth, and I smiled.

Some people refer to their spouse as their better half. Or their good right arm. John is more like my right arm and left arm and both legs combined. Not my soul mate, but my soul itself.

Teaching is not a 9 to 5 job. It follows teachers home at night and pervades their existence. From the mountains of paperwork to making phone calls to writing lesson plans, the weight of keeping up can be oppressive. Don't get me wrong. I loved it. But I would not have been the teacher I was without John's support.

I have no sense of direction. I always told people it was because I was a breech birth. Before the invention of GPS, this would pose a problem when I made home visits in the early days of my career. John would make me a paper map, with hand drawn pictures of landmarks, and the night before a scheduled visit, he would accompany me on a practice run as I would navigate my way from the school parking lot to the designated student's home.

After receiving a couple technology grants, I got two computers for my students to use. The kids and I were thrilled to get them, but I had no separate desks to put them on, and the space in my tiny bathroom was limited. John bought some shelving materials at Home Depot. One day after working all night at the bakery, he came in and built me a computer station that fit in the space available. I remember being proud of the kids for ignoring the distraction and working on their assignments that day. Several of them even made a point of thanking him when he left.

Principal Grover floated the idea of having a spaghetti dinner one year before Open House conferences. Knowing that John had managed an Italian restaurant for several years, I mentioned it to him, and he readily volunteered to organize it. It was very successful, and repeated for several years thereafter.

When I directed *L'il Abner,* a friend put me in touch with a pig farmer. Most directors use a stuffed toy, but that wasn't good enough for me. John drove to the farm to pick the piggy up one Sunday morning when I was at church. The beastie lived in my garage for the performance week of the show, and every morning John would get up and slop the pig. Every night John loaded Snorky . . . he had to have a name for the program . . . into his crate and I would drive to school, where one of my students would unload him. The pig did his two scenes with Moonbeam McSwine and returned home with me, where my husband would return him to the haven of our garage. That's when my friend Joanne started referring to me as "the *first* Mrs. Carroll."

I don't know how many times John listened to me vent, or cry, or laugh, or curse my fool head off. Or how many times he held me in his arms and held me together. I *did* know I was blessed every day I woke up next to him. *How did I get so lucky?*

. . . " blah blah blah blah, Miss Carroll?" I came out of my fog and looked at Mrs. Charleston. She was standing next to me, holding a tray full of individual pieces of graduation cake. There were forks stuck into the pieces.

"I'm sorry, I was lost in thought."

"Would you like a piece of cake?" she repeated. She was making the rounds with the dessert.

"Yes, thank you. It looks delicious."

"Me, too," said John.

She set down two pieces of cake and smiled at me. "One for you, one for your cabana boy."

Train Story

As much as I loved working with the kids, I confess that I looked forward to my vacations. It was nice to think about lying under a beach umbrella or seeing Mickey Mouse when winter dragged on in Central New York. One school year we saved a pile of money so we could head overseas during the summer break.

It was a whole lot of years ago. I know John and I were both MUCH younger. Our knees were healthy and our sense of adventure was strong. We started off in London with our backpacks and our BritRail passes, and we knocked around the British Isles for three weeks. After seeing Buckingham Palace, the Tower of London, and Stonehenge, we moved on to Scotland where we did *not* find the Loch Ness Monster.

Eventually we boarded a train heading south. It was an all-day trip that would eventually take us to the port of Holyhead in Wales where we would catch a ferry to Ireland. That was the plan anyway.

I remember the scenery was raw and ruggedly beautiful. Rolling green hills that went on and on. And cows. Lots of cows. So here we were, on the last day of our train passes, headed out of Britain and across the sea to Ireland.

John, who never met a man he didn't like, struck up a conversation with an elderly gentleman across the aisle. Grandpa Joe was from the American Midwest, and he was a colorful character. Fiercely independent, he was a WWII vet who had lost an arm in the war. He wore coke bottle glasses that made his eyes look humongous. He was traveling with his granddaughter, and as it turned out, they were *also* headed for the ferry to Ireland. The granddaughter was perhaps 17 or 18, and she wasn't so much drop dead gorgeous as she was "farmer's daughter" pretty, and exceedingly flirtatious. Between the blond hair, the long eyelashes, and the American Midwest accent, Flirty had the Scottish boys drooling in their haggis. She had slightly less luggage than Imelda Marcos had shoes.

So there we were, chatting away with our American neighbors when the train stopped. No warning, no announcement about coming into a station, just . . . stopped. I looked out the window. A cow looked back at me. We were in a farmer's pasture. I didn't think much of it until the wait went on for a while. There didn't appear to be anyone working on fixing anything. I put my nose in my book. Time ticked away. We started to grow concerned about making our connections. Things had to line up perfectly. We had to get off in Crewe and change trains to get to Holyhead, and then catch the 3 p.m. ferry for Ireland. Our rail passes were due to expire at midnight. We already had ferry tickets. We had reservations at a bed & breakfast in Dublin.

A conductor came through the car and told us there was a rail strike. Whatever the deadline for the engineers was, it had passed, and in unison around the country, they had pulled their brakes and shut down their trains. Management was calling in some high-level suits to substitute for the engineers. They would be arriving . . . well, they would be arriving sometime. I pulled the conductor aside and spoke with him privately.

"We aren't going to make our connection in Crewe, are we? My husband and I have to get to Holyhead in time to get on the ferry to Dublin. We've already got tickets."

He smiled at me sympathetically and pulled a train schedule out of his back pocket and looked at it. "If we get moving soon, there is a train going through Chester that will take you to Holyhead. The problem is, you will only have about two minutes to make your move. This train will pull into Chester for a brief stop, and you will have to find out if the train to Holyhead has already gone through. With this delay, I don't know if we will get there in time or not. You will have to find a conductor there and ask him."

Shortly after that our train started moving again. John and I made our plans with Grandpa Joe and Flirty. I was the teacher with the big voice, so I would hop off the train in Chester and pounce on an authority figure. John would wait by the door with our new friends and the luggage. I would either wave them on or hop back on the train.

We pulled into Chester. I burst off the train. "Has the train to Holyhead gone through?" The first person I asked might have been a four-year-old child, I don't remember. I repeated myself, over and over again, with my voice getting louder and louder. *Why were people staring at me? It was a simple enough question. Was that man wearing . . . a BritRail uniform?* I just about tackled him.

"Has the train to Holyhead gone through yet?"

"No." He wasn't too pleased with the crazed tourist standing in front of him.

Like Secretariat at the Belmont, I thundered back to the train.

"John! It's a go! Get off the train! Get off the train! Get off the . . ."

If only he could have gotten off the train. While I had been playing the captain of the Spanish Inquisition, people from Chester were boarding the train. John was wearing his backpack, and carrying mine, which I had stupidly left on board. He is a big man to begin with and encumbered by two packs and a crowd of passengers moving against the tide, he was having difficulty moving forward. And that wasn't the only problem. Flirty had a plethora of luggage. Grandpa Joe had one arm, and he couldn't see past his nose. How was he going to navigate the threshold of the train car and step safely onto the platform? Flirty's arms were full, and John was now kicking more of her bags out the doorway. I took Grandpa Joe by the one good arm and guided his steps. A young man with a long face hung his head out the train window.

"Where are you going?" he asked me.

"To Ireland, I hope."

We had a brief wait while we caught our breath. Grandpa Joe said there were other people on our train that had plans to go to Holyhead that hadn't gotten off when we did.

"They are going to be out of luck. Too bad they don't have our ingenuity," he said. I asked our traveling companions to pose while I snapped their picture in Chester. I certainly wanted to remember them.

The train for Holyhead arrived, and we piled aboard. There were literally no seats available, so we sat on our luggage in the aisle of one of the cars. We were in a smoking cab. It was hot, and it stunk, and I didn't even care. We would make our connection. Flirty even found a new group of young men to fawn over her.

We *did* get to Holyhead in time, and we did make our connecting ferry. Another couple hours across the sea and we would be in Ireland where a bed, and dinner somewhere, awaited. The ferry was pretty empty, so we had our pick of seats. We stowed the backpacks overhead and settled in. And we waited. And we waited. And the intercom system came on.

"Ladies and Gentlemen, we regret to tell you that our trip today will be delayed. Due to today's rail strike, we are waiting for passengers from a train that got stuck near Crewe."

John smiled at me as he reclined his chair. "I think it's time for my nap," he said.

Descent

Typically by the second week in August, I started looking forward to the start of a new school year. I always enjoyed picking out new school supplies. I stocked up at Staples when they had their one-cent pocket folder sale. They limited you to ten folders, but if you dragged your husband with you, you could get twenty of them, and if you went back the next day you could get twenty more. I admit, I was apprehensive about the changes at Baldwin, but I had had a nice break, and I was rested. I decided I would just focus on the kids in my room and enjoy my time with them. I could do this. Or so I thought.

We barely got started before the temperature in the frog pot kicked up again. The beginning of the school year typically started with lots of paperwork for staff and students. The third day of classes, we ran out of copy paper. Teachers scrambled for overheads and transparencies and had kids copy information off their overhead projector screens. At the first professional development session after school, we were told that administrators would be coming to visit classes. They were expecting to see a couple techniques that had been promoted during our summer training. A *do-it-now* (DIN) was a quick 3-5 question review of the previous lesson. A *ticket-out-the-door* (TOTD) was given at the end of the class period. It was a quick review of what had happened during class.

Question: "How can I do DINS and TOTD without paper?"

(Translation: "Am I to make bricks without straw?")

Answer: "We have confidence in you."

After a week or so, more paper arrived. Sarah, the copy technician, was back churning out copies. Two days later, we ran out of copy machine ink, which brought things to a standstill once again.

Around this time, an email came out from the administrator who was in charge of getting teachers paid for our summer professional development. Even though we were originally told all we had to do was sign the sign-in sheet, now we needed to fill out a time card. See the attachment for directions about how to fill out the time card. Time cards were available in the main office.

An hour later, there was another email. We were out of time cards.

Still, we pushed on. One afternoon, Hannah, a math teacher, came to see me about one of my resource students. She had used one of the *new techniques* being preached from our *new Bible*. A "cold call" was when a teacher asked a question, and then followed it with the name of the student who was to answer. Instead of saying, "John, would you please read the first paragraph," you would say "Read the first paragraph for us . . . John." The idea is that since no one knew who was going to be called on, everyone paid closer attention.

Hannah was being observed the day she "cold called" one of my resource students to read out loud. The student refused. Hannah persisted. The student refused again. I explained to Hannah that you cannot demand that a kid with a reading disability read out loud in class without time to review the material. He knows he doesn't read well. He does not want to be embarrassed in front of his peers. "But they are observing us for these techniques," Hannah said to me.

"They are not going to see them in my room," I answered her. *Even dog trainers say the name of the dog before giving a command,* I thought.

On a positive note, Principal Len had switched me to another administrator for future evaluations, but Miss Lucy was still the administrator in charge of resource students, and I still had to interact with her. At our first department meeting, she started banging away on her metaphorical drum. She reminded us that all resource teachers must do daily lessons that reinforce the requirements of Regents exams. I started reviewing my students' folders to see what exams they needed for graduation. Then I looked at students' schedules to see when they were scheduled with me, and realized there were very few cases where students in the same resource class needed the same exam. I had expected this. Grouping students by the same grade does not ensure that they have "similar needs." *I told you so, Miss Lucy.*

I would not be able to do group instruction; instead, I made up activity packets for kids that were tailored to their individual exams. *Marty, here's a practice document-based question. Read the first two pages and answer the questions that follow. When that is finished, you can start your algebra homework. Let me know if I can help you.* Marty hated it. Like other returning Baldwin students, he was used to using his resource time to get the help he needed. His math homework was due the next day. He saw no point in starting prep for a June Regents when it was September. I felt like an ass insisting that he comply with my idiotic request.

About four weeks into the school year, I became aware of another uptick in the temperature in my frog pot. It started with TMJ in my jaw. The nightmares started. I wasn't sleeping well at night, and I woke up every morning at 5 a.m. with my heart hammering in my chest. I had chronic diarrhea. Migraine headaches, which I hadn't had since my sister died of Lou Gehrig's disease, had returned. My stomach felt tight and knotted. I was nauseous every morning before school. On some days, I was vomiting up my breakfast. I was aware that my breathing was restricted. I didn't want to socialize. Weekends were spent worrying about going in on Monday morning. Simple tasks seemed very difficult. I told friends that I "missed myself." What was wrong with me?

Just before Columbus Day, we had our Open House. Parents came by in the evening to meet their children's teachers and talk about course requirements. M'Kiwa Walker, now a senior, and her mom, stopped by my room. I loved M'Kiwa. I loved her mom. M'Kiwa had worked hard, and was due to graduate in June. Mom had some questions about required courses and college applications. It was a very upbeat conversation, but at some point, I realized I wasn't there. My mouth was moving, and words were coming out, but I was watching the conversation from above, like a story you hear about people who die on the operating table and watch the doctors doing CPR before they are brought back to life.

It scared the bejesus out of me.

I made an appointment with a therapist I had previously seen when my sister Pat was dying. Janelle told me I had some symptoms of Complex Post Traumatic Stress Disorder.

PTSD? From teaching? Nobody gets PTSD from teaching. Soldiers on a battlefield get PTSD.

I called a friend when I got home. Sterling had served in Vietnam when he was just 18, and he developed PTSD from his experience there. He was the new kid on patrol when his Jeep hit a land mine. The Jeep overturned. Snipers picked off everyone else in the Jeep. Sterling survived because he was the only one wearing a flak vest. Sterling told me that PTSD was not only experienced by battlefield veterans. It can be brought on by a single traumatic event, like a bad car crash or a house fire. In addition, another form, called Complex PTSD, can be brought on by long-term traumatic events such as recurring domestic violence, childhood soldiering, or captivity.

Captivity?

Yes, captivity, like POWS, or sweatshop workers, or concentration camp survivors, or people who escape from a cult. People who are stuck in an environment *where they have no control.*

I hung up the phone and got on the computer. I typed in teachers with PTSD. And ping, ping, ping. The articles started popping up. Stories about teachers who were overregulated, overextended, and overstressed. Stories about teachers who had faced years of dealing with the fallout of student poverty, societal violence, pressure to raise test scores, teacher bashing, lack of parental support, lack of funding, and *lack of autonomy.* Symptoms of Complex PTSD included persistent sadness or explosive anger, headaches, chest pain, stomach aches, feelings of helplessness, loss of concentration, disassociation, hyperarousal, and relationship problems. Alcohol or drug abuse and suicidal thoughts can follow.

This is a real thing? It has a name? Holy shit.

I made an appointment to see my doctor. Could he prescribe a medication to help me get through this?

"I'd advise against it, Pam," he told me. "With the level of stress you are experiencing, it would take a significant amount of meds. You would become a different person."

"Really?" I asked him.

"You would be . . . flat. You would have no affect at all. How about a medical leave? Do you have paid sick time?"

"Yes. Quite a bit." I answered him.

"I would rather do that. Let's start with eight weeks. Then we will meet again and re-evaluate."

I looked at him and sighed. "I don't know."

"I have written several of these leaves for teachers in the last few years. What is going on in the schools?" he asked me.

Was I really going to do this? Was I going to walk away? It's not what I wanted. Not how I planned to end my career at Baldwin. I knew a couple people who had gone out on leave from the district, and that was fine for them, but not for me.

I was a rock. I would not let this defeat me. I would pull myself up by my bootstraps. I would endure. I would . . . I would . . . I would fall apart if I didn't get out of there. Did I want to walk out, or get carried out?

Holy Shit! How did I get in this pot of boiling water?

So, on a Tuesday morning in October, I called in sick. Paperwork from the doctor in hand, I snuck into my room at o-dark-thirty like some type of secret agent. I wrote letters to the kids explaining that my elderly parents were aging rapidly, and that I wanted to spend more time with them. (It was the truth, if not the whole truth.) I grabbed my laptop, a few files, and a couple special pigs that were sitting on a shelf. I filled up the snack basket with granola bars. I organized my planning folder with several weeks of Regents exam practice lessons for a substitute. I turned off the light, and I locked the door. It was so easy. And it wasn't.

I dropped the letters for the kids in the outgoing mail bin in the office. Some of the early-bird teachers were starting to arrive. I sought out a handful of coworker friends to speak with personally. Each of them was at first, quite surprised, and then very supportive. You must take care of yourself first, they told me.

Then I went to see Principal Len. I told him I was taking some time off. I gave him my doctor's paperwork. He was floored. After he collected himself, he told me if he and I were to die on the job, someone from the district would push our dead bodies out of the way, step over top of us, and plant another person in our chairs. I stood up to leave, fighting back the tears. He got out of his chair, walked around his desk and hugged me.

Would I teach again? I'd miss it terribly. Teaching fed my soul. In the grand scheme of things, however, I was only one teacher, and as Rick told Ilsa on that airport runway in *Casablanca*, the problems of little people don't add up to a hill of beans in this crazy world. A bigger problem looms for America's educators. Until this country begins to value education for all of our children, and demands the changes necessary, we are merely rearranging the deck chairs on the Titanic.

I hope I live to see it.

Dog Park

It was very strange being home during school hours. I felt like I was playing hooky, and had a big case of the guilts about it. My schedule had changed so abruptly. I found myself looking for ways to fill my time. John was working nights at a bakery, and when he got home in the morning at ten or eleven, we often put Pinky in her crate and drove over to our local dog park. A group of us had formed sort of a canine play group. We had a standing date three times a week when some or all of us brought our four-legged friends for a good romp and ourselves for a good conversation.

Eleanor was Getta's human. And before you ask, I will tell you that Getta was named Getta because Eleanor's husband said they just *had to get-a*-dog. Eleanor was a retired kindergarten teacher who took an interest in me and asked how it was possible that I could go to the park during school hours. So I told her. I had decided early on that I would answer the why-are-you-on-leave question with honesty. Other school teachers understand the stress of a career in education better than non-teachers. I suppose the same is true for physicians, or iron workers, or post office workers who go postal. Eleanor was a great listener at a time when I needed to heal.

She told me she always wanted to write a book about her career in teaching, and I told her I was already at work on one. In conversation that day, I told her the story of Alan, and after she nearly wet her pants laughing, Eleanor told me I *must* put it in my book. So here it is:

I was Molly's co-teacher in different science classes for many years. Our teaching styles complemented each other very well. In a lot of ways we were alike, but we had our differences as well. She wouldn't say shit if she had a mouthful, and I, well . . . I walked around a lot of the time with my foot in my mouth. Part of the 9th grade General Science curriculum was the reproductive system. Male diagram. Female diagram. The journey of the egg. The journey of the sperm. Fertilization in the fallopian tube. Development of the fetus. I always enjoyed teaching this unit because the kids were always interested in it. Some parents are comfortable telling their children about the birds and the bees with great clarity, but others are not. I always encouraged the kids to ask questions about anything. "I want you to have correct information," I told them. "Ask me *anything* you want to know. "

Can you get pregnant if you do it standing up?

If it is your first time?

If you use Coca Cola afterwards?

One brave young woman asked if she could get pregnant if she . . . swallowed. It took me a moment to understand the question. It took her classmates only a bit longer, and then the shrieking started.

I can't believe you asked that!

Oh, my God!

What are you, stupid?

I answered the question by reviewing the pathway of the digestive tract and making note of which parts are connected to what. I reminded the kids that the digestive tract and the reproductive system do not intersect. I told them there is no such thing as a stupid question, and repeated that I would rather that they have accurate information. "I have been teaching for many years. You cannot embarrass me. It cannot be done."

I quickly learned that it can be *very* embarrassing for students to ask such intimate questions in front of their peers. In subsequent teachings of this lesson, I suggested that the kids write down their questions on a piece of paper and leave them on my desk as they exited the classroom. During the next class I could address them to the entire class and their anonymity would be maintained. That system worked well until the year that Alan joined our class. Even though the notes were not signed, I recognized the handwriting.

Does pussy taste good?

Ok, I thought, this was not a real question. This was Alan being Alan. How am I going to handle this? I suppose I could have ignored it, but that didn't feel right. I did, after all, tell them they could ask *anything*. I approached Alan when he entered the room at the start of the next class.

"Alan," I said, extending my right hand. "I want to congratulate you." He took my hand and shook it.

"Why?"

"Because you did it. After all my many years of teaching, you managed to embarrass me with your question. Congratulations. Oh, and the answer to your question is, I don't know. I've never tried it. You will have to ask someone else."

His face blazed red. His friend Dan looked at him. "What did you ask her?"

I looked at Dan. "He asked me if pussy tastes good."

Dan smacked Alan on the back of the head and barked, "You idiot!"

I turned my head so they couldn't see me smile.

A few days after I told Eleanor the Alan story, John and Pinky and I returned to the dog park. The temperature on the previous visit was about ninety, and the dogs were quite lethargic. On this beautiful fall day, about sixty-five degrees, they were making up for lost time. Petunia, a French bulldog, found a deflated rubber football and was chasing it all over the park. Several of the humans were seated on two benches and their dogs, as was typical, decided to play under and around the benches where the people were seated. For reasons unknown to moi, they are completely uninterested in the empty benches elsewhere in the park.

I was sitting next to some of the other humans when Harrigan (a large, lanky, goofy Red Bone Coon Hound) decided to wrestle with both Nestle (chocolate lab) and Lily (pit lab mix) under the bench. Harrigan thoroughly enjoyed gumming Lily's neck while uttering the *aroooo- roo - rooing* sound common to hounds. This went on for a few minutes, and after getting whacked in the legs with this dog's head and that dog's body rump, I attempted to break them up by imitating a cat noise. Harrigan left Lily alone to go and find said cat. We all . . . including Harrigan's human . . . laughed at the dog's apparent inability to discern between a real cat and my lame imitation of one.

After a few minutes of fruitless hunting, Harrigan returned to chomp on Lily's neck some more, except that he misjudged the distance and chomped on my inner thigh instead. Fortunately there was no damage done, as he was not using teeth. I popped up from the bench and decided to give the beasties some space while I massaged my thigh and told

Harrigan to stay away from my bikini line. Mortified, Harrigan's human came over to see if I was ok.

"Yes, Matt, I am fine. I was just not expecting that." At which point, my husband said . . .

"Harrigan is just looking for the kitty."

Decades later that wonderful man still makes me laugh every day.

Alan would have loved it.

Affirmation

I never did go back to Baldwin High School. I took those first eight weeks off and realized I would self-destruct if I tried to return. It took me a long, long time and many sessions with Janelle, my therapist, to detox from my experiences there. Early on, she had told me it would be at least a year until I felt like myself again. It wasn't until I left that toxic environment and looked at it in the rear-view mirror that I saw it for what it was. My PTSD was not something I would "get over," Janelle had told me. I would have to examine it piece by piece and learn to integrate it into my psyche.

I spent the next several months focusing on myself and healing. A few people asked why I just didn't go work in another school, but they didn't realize how wounded I was. I was required to see Doctor Dalton every six weeks and have him renew my medical leave paperwork. I met Janelle twice a month. Some sessions were harder than others. It was painful for me to learn I was replaceable. As Principal Len had predicted, Baldwin High School somehow continued to function without me. I had wrestled with perfectionism in the past, and now I had to come to terms with the fact that I was not infallible. It was a humbling experience for me.

I decided I would retire at the end of that school year. Teachers traditionally retire in June. It's easier for the district and better for the kids to have a new teacher in place when school restarts in September. The April after I left, I contacted my union president to start the retirement paperwork, but I learned I could not officially retire until my 55th birthday, which was not until the following December. *I had already waited six months. Would I ever be free?* I had more than enough years of experience, and still had plenty of sick days, but I wasn't old enough to collect a pension. John and I considered my just resigning and living off our savings for a while, but then we would lose our health insurance. I would have to wait it out. Never patient with myself, I didn't want to hear that. I wanted to be done with it.

My union president advised me to continue to use my sick days. I had plenty of them. "Let the district pay your salary. You can go from medical leave to retirement. You earned it," he told me. "Try to relax."

Relax? I thought. That's not gonna happen. Not till I'm really done.

I continued to work with Janelle. Session by session, she gently prodded me, and session by session, I slogged my way to recovery. As the months passed and time finally got short, I started to feel positively giddy. It was like I was five years old with Christmas coming. I told Janelle I could see the checkered flag. Since I was planning to retire the day after my 55th birthday, she started to push me to have a birthday/retirement party. Several friends had also suggested it, but I had resisted. Considering it had been such a long time since I had seen many folks from school, considering I had slunk out the door on that Tuesday morning, considering I had been out on medical leave instead of finishing the race, I had the idea that I did not deserve a party. Silly, I know, but that's how I felt at the time.

When Janelle said it would be good closure for me, I decided she was right. John was the one who told me my party could take any form I wanted it to. I could invite *only* those people I wanted to. I didn't have to have one of those quickie parties held after school in the teachers' lounge where *people-you-recognize-as-employees-in-your-building-but-whose-names-you-don't-know* stop by for a piece of cake. Gatherings where everyone looks at their watch and wonders when they can gracefully leave were not my idea of fun. I much preferred the retirement parties I had attended off campus.

I came up with a list of friends from home and from school and invited them for dinner at one of my favorite restaurants. We had a private room, and offered five entrée choices for our guests to pick from. John and his boss at the bakery made a fabulous vanilla sheet cake with pink frosting, which I decorated with home-made fondant piggies. I made giant frosted piggy cookies as table favors, one for each place setting. The room was very pretty. It was the first week of December, so there were green garlands and twinkling lights everywhere. Everything was ready, but I was oddly nervous waiting for folks to arrive. Would they have a good time? Did they really want to be here? People started arriving ... and it was as if no time had passed.

"You look fabulous," Geena said, hugging me as she entered the room. "I know you said no presents, but I couldn't resist this little trinket." She handed me a cute little tissue wrapped gift. I opened it to find a piggy Christmas ornament.

"I'm so happy for you," Karen smiled at me as she took my hand. "Congratulations."

One friend after another approached me with smiling faces and arms wide open. The noise level grew and the waitresses finally had to urge us to take our seats so they could serve dinner. I felt like the Queen of England. Where was my royal scepter?

My friend Roy approached me. "Pammy!" he said, licking crumbs off his face. "Do you have any more of those pig cookies? They are delicious!"

I gave Roy a couple extra cookies I had brought along in case any of them broke on the way to the restaurant, and he snarfed them down. Then he went from person to person with dollar bills, offering to buy *their* cookies.

After dinner, my teaching partner Molly said some kind words. Tim, another resource teacher, presented me with an honorary Baldwin High School Diploma. I was presented with a "perpetual hall pass," which was constructed out of plastic, glitter, and golden Christmas tinsel, which gave me permission to go to the bathroom *"immediately, when I actually had to go,"* as well as *"eat in a leisurely manner and actually digest my food."* In a room full of schoolteachers, no one was shy about public speaking. We laughed ourselves silly.

As John and I packed up the car that night with leftover cake and an arm full of "Happy Birthday/Happy Retirement" cards, I was riding high. It finally broke through my thick skull that Janelle was right all along . . . this was *fabulous* closure. Nobody cared about how I had left Baldwin.

They only cared about *me.*

Home

After my retirement party, I spent the rest of the winter sleeping late, reading, and gazing at the snow fall. There is something very decadent about watching school buses drive through sloppy slush while you snuggle on the couch under a blanket, pet the cat, and have another cup of coffee. Spring came and I began volunteering at our zoo. A few times I traveled with a zoo staffer on a field trip. We packed up animals and brought them to a local library for a sort of a show-and-tell for young children. In July, I spent two weeks as an assistant in a zoo camp for 5th graders. We went to animal demonstrations, learned about different habitats, and played some zoo games. It was fun, but it also made me realize how much I missed working with kids. I was tired of being retired.

Jackie, one of my former colleagues, had recommended that I look into tutoring at our local community college. She retired several years before I did, and had been teaching and tutoring there part-time for a while.

"You would *love* it," she told me, "and they would love you."

It was the middle of August when I looked up the website and poked around the employment section. I found a listing for professional reading tutors. I filled out the paperwork, rewrote my decades-old resume, and hit the send button. If it wasn't the *very* next day, it was the day after that that I got a phone call from the head of the reading department. She wanted me to come in for an interview.

"When can you come in? What day is good for you? Bring your passport."

My passport? Umm, OK. When I walked into the reading office a few days later, I ran smack into Jackie, the friend who had suggested I fill out an application. I told her I was there for an interview, and she said she was going to start praying immediately. I have great friends.

Phones were ringing, people were milling about, and things were very busy. It was typical week-before-school-opens activity. The reading director, Donna, gave me a brief description of the job. She said that due to budgetary constraints, I would have to work with *two* or even *three* students at a time. I managed to keep a straight face and told her that would be fine, all the while remembering the time I had eleven kids crammed in my tiny bathroom taking the English Regents for six hours. Then Donna put a blank Monday - Friday tutoring schedule in front of me and asked me to fill in the times that I was available.

"So I'm in?"

"You're in. You were in when I read your resume."

Somebody wants me?

Somebody values my experience?

The passport she asked me to bring? It was the preferred ID to start a background check. Donna told me to go to the human resources department to fill out the new-hire paperwork. It was that easy.

A few days later, I attended a welcome-to-a-new-semester meeting for the members of the department. On my way upstairs, I stopped in the bathroom, and of all things to focus on, I noticed the toilet paper. No one had stolen the toilet paper. The water faucets were the automatic kind, and a bit of spray collected on the sides of the sink as I washed my hands. I found myself using a piece of paper towel to mop up the excess. It was so clean and pretty, and I just wanted to . . . preserve it.

I left the bathroom and walked past the café where a few students were gathering. No bells were ringing. No announcements were blaring over the intercom. No one was running in the hall. No F bombs assaulted my ears. I went to the reading lab and walked in. Smiling women welcomed me. One had brought applesauce cake. Director Donna detailed some pertinent issues and we went around the table introducing ourselves. I told them that I had retired, but was now back working part time because I really missed the kids. Heads nodded.

Was I in Stepford?

Just before Labor Day, I started tutoring in the reading lab. The very first student I met on opening day was a Baldwin graduate. Trevor had been one of Theresa's resource kids, and he was as nervous as I was about starting a new adventure. I had been at Baldwin a long time. I was used to being the one who people sought out when they had a question or were unfamiliar with a process. Asking for help with a new routine was unfamiliar territory for me. I was out of my element, as was Trevor who was now a freshman all over again. I told Trevor we could figure it out together, and that we would both be fine in a couple weeks. I was right.

My first year at the community college went very smoothly. Oh, sure, some kids didn't turn in their assignments, and copy machines occasionally broke down. But everyone in the reading lab was professional, courteous, and willing to help me out when I had questions. I loved the job and I was good at it. We ate a lot of Dove Chocolates and I entertained my new coworkers with Baldwin stories. I felt like Deborah Kerr in *From Here to Eternity*... I never knew it could be like this.

After a couple years of sheer bliss, one of the higher ups decided to move the tutors who were scattered across campus under one communal roof. I guess it made sense of some sort. It meant the students now had one central location where they could get whatever help they needed. But like many new programs, our foray into the new tutoring center had some kinks that hadn't been worked out yet.

I didn't care much for the design. Alternating glass panels of pale turquoise and day-glo orange hung down from the ceiling, lengthwise, dividing the room into two sections. Small offices with computers were on the left side of the glass partition. The tutoring area was on the right side with assorted arrangements of tables and chairs. Some of the chairs were standard office chairs - also in day-glo orange - but more than half of them were stools on casters which were covered in avocado green or burnt orange vinyl. We referred to them, not fondly, as "tuffets." Young men with long legs found their chins almost resting on their knees. Young ladies in shorter skirts could not straddle them without exposing themselves.

Noise became an issue. A math tutor would naturally raise his voice as he stepped away from his students and began working at a nearby white board. It was not unreasonable, but it was difficult for the reading tutor at a table next to him who was trying to quietly read a chapter with her students.

Then there were the oblivious adults who willingly discussed any personal item at the top of their voices in detailed minutia. My least favorite was the science tutor who laughed constantly. Like a hyena.

We were a couple months into the semester when things started to really go askew at our new location. Between the ridiculous chairs, the noise, and the unprofessional professionals, the stress was returning to my life. One morning eight or so adults came in carrying cameras, sound equipment, a wardrobe rack, and an air brush machine to film a television commercial. They parked themselves on the left side of the room, clogging up the aisle by the small computer offices. One of the gentlemen in the group moved to a table near me, pulled out his cell phone, and began a lengthy and loud conversation.

Other tutors and students were irritated, and distracted by the intrusion, but I was becoming apoplectic. At one point I looked down and saw that my fists were clenched together.

My breathing was rapid and shallow. I was becoming enraged. What was the matter with me?

And a little voice said, *this is your PTSD, Pammy. Get out of here. Go take a walk.*

I looked at the clock. My students wouldn't be arriving for another twenty minutes, so I stood up and headed down the stairs. I left the tutoring center, and then strode down the hall and opened the outside door of the building. Descending the front steps, I turned and headed for the other side of the quad, and sat down on one of the benches. Students were ambling in different directions. The sun was shining. I stayed a few minutes, and then returned to the tutoring center.

I spoke with the director of the center, who told me they were filming a promo commercial for the college. She did ask them to quiet down, and they complied. And yes, I understand that a college must do some self-promotion to keep enrollment up. I knew I had overreacted. But you can't tell a Vietnam vet that the noise he hears is just a car backfiring, because by the time you get the words out, he is already under the table ducking for cover. I just could not work in chaos anymore. *Damn it.*

I was used to tilting at windmills, so I did not really expect much of a reaction when I sent out an email to the other reading tutors. I wanted to know if *my* concerns about the constant noise and interruptions and unprofessional behavior were the concerns of others as well, and asked if they were willing to meet to discuss possible solutions. The response was overwhelming and gratifying. Everyone was on the same page. We met with our reading director, who in turn met with the president of the college the next day, and then immediately began work on a proposal that would move us out of the larger tutoring center into a space of our own that was right next door. *Oh, please, oh please.*

November arrived and the semester was flying by. Kids were working to get caught up with their assignments and get their portfolios in order. Computers were in high demand.

There were five desktop models, all of them on the second floor. They were each located inside an individual computer office which had floor to ceiling windows and glass doors. To be fair, there were also a good number of laptops available, but alas, they were not connected to the printer. I had little patience for the English tutors who would camp out in the private computer rooms drinking coffee, grading papers, and surfing the net while they would wait . . . and wait . . . and wait for a *potential* student to show up who may or may not need computer access. It was infuriating.

One morning Cora, another reading tutor, approached me and said she had a kid who needed a computer. She had asked one of the English tutors to vacate the small computer office and the tutor had refused. Maybe it was the phase of the moon, or maybe it was approaching winter solstice, but I had had enough. My "inner Baldwin" was rising to the surface. I told Cora to come with me. A brunette English tutor was grading papers as we approached her open door.

"Hi, I see you have no students. I have a kid who needs a computer, so I need to ask you to leave this room for a little while."

"Well, OK, but you need to understand I have a student coming."

"She will just be a minute," Cora interjected. "She needs to type a cover page."

Esme, Cora's student, entered the computer room and looked at the brunette English tutor. Sucking her teeth, she said, "I'm only gonna be a *minute*." Brunette English Tutor quickly scurried from the room. The student typed her cover page and left. Brunette English Tutor returned.

An hour passed. Another reading tutor, Marianne, approached me. "Pam, I need your help. I'm such a wuss. I have a kid who needs a computer. Will you help me?"

Once again, I was on my feet. "Don't boot the brunette. We booted her last time." I approached a blond English tutor, who was encamped in another one of the private computer rooms. She saw me coming and started in before I could say hello.

"I got here early this morning so I could set up in my office," she barked at me.

Standing in the doorway, I dramatically leaned to my right and looked for a non-existent name plate next to the door frame. "I wasn't aware that this was *your* office."

"I may have a student coming in twenty minutes," She peered at me over the top of her reading glasses. There was a newspaper spread out in front of her with a half-eaten muffin on top. A half full mug of coffee was set to the side.

May have? I smiled at her. "Well, a student in the hand is worth two in the bush."

It was if she had no idea how to respond. She got up on her feet. "I am going to see the director about this."

I continued to smile. "I think that's a great idea. Should I come with you?"

She stormed off. From somewhere across the tutoring center, a student said, "Go, Miss Pam!"

Marianne's student entered the office to do her assignment. I returned to my table.

Several minutes later, Blond English Tutor returned from downstairs, and approached me. "I talked to the director. There are laptops available that the students can use."

"Well, that's true, but they aren't connected to the printers. Can you sit down a minute?" I asked her. *Maybe I could make her understand this.*

"No, I have a student. I was working the other day and a student came in and interrupted me and asked to use the computer. That was offensive. It is offensive of you to 'boot me' out of that office."

"You said you were in *your* office."

"Semantics? We're going to talk about semantics? I find that offensive."

I stood up and looked at her, eye level. "Well, right now, I find *you* offensive." Her mouth fell open.

She finally shut up. As she quickly made her exit, I said, "See? We agree on something."

It might have been two or three days after my *offensive* conversation with Blond English Tutor that we got the word from our reading director . . . we were moving. We were moving immediately. Into our own space next door. Into a sort of an annex to the tutoring center. Better for us. Better for the math folks that would be moving into the larger center next semester. Better for the English tutors who wouldn't have to share space with us.

We were in our new place by early December. The furniture and computers from our original site were brought over. The semester was drawing to a close and it was crunch time for the kids. Many were coming in for extra sessions. We were crazy busy, but we were happy because we were a community again. I must have been feeling philosophical, because I had rather a profound thought. Was it possible my PTSD was a gift? Sort of an early warning system? An alarm that squawked, "Hey, Froggy! Do not get into another pot of boiling water!"

I knew for a lot of people who had it, PTSD was a curse. It could be crippling and prevent them from doing things they wanted or needed to do. But in my case, perhaps it was time to embrace my PTSD. It had reared its head when I needed it to. It nipped at my heels and told me to protect myself from another negative environment. I should be grateful. Maybe I should get down on my knees and give thanks for it.

Winter had arrived, and the temperature dropped. There was no place for coats in our new annex space, so I offered to bring a coatrack I had used at Baldwin High. Years and years ago, my friend Joanne had advised me to label every piece of furniture in my little bathroom. "Take a piece of masking tape and write down your name and your room number. Then when everything goes into the hallway for summer cleaning, it will be easier for the custodians to know what belongs back in your room."

A few days later, I carried in the coatrack from the car, and I noticed the masking tape label from Baldwin was still there: "Carroll - 200." I walked down the hallway and opened the door to our new space. The name plate read "Reading Lab - 200". Well, look at that. After all the drama of the last few years, I had found my way home.

And you know what Dorothy said about that.

Made in United States
North Haven, CT
18 December 2021

13153470R00176